Praying the Prayer of the Church

The psalmists display a passionate concern for the poor, the needy and the outcasts. All proceeds from this book will go to THOMAS (Those On the Margin of Society), an organisation which shares in practical fashion that concern of the psalmists.

Praying the Prayer of the Church

Richard Atherton

Redemptorist Publications
Alphonsus House, Chawton, Hants GU34 3HQ

First printed February 1998

Cover illustration: Angus Mewse
Design: Maureen Francis

ISBN 0 85231 174 5

Printed in Britain by:
Optichrome The Printing Group, Woking, Surrey, GU21 5HX

Contents

Introduction

I read about him recently. Graham works in a garage; one day he called into a religious bookshop and asked if they had a cheap edition of the Prayer of the Church. 'You see,' he said by way of explanation, 'I take it with me to work, and it gets awful greasy!' Graham had learned the lesson that many have yet to learn: that the Prayer of the Church is for everyone – including car mechanics. Indeed, one of the achievements of the Church in modern times has been the practical recognition that the Office, or Prayer of the Church, belongs to the whole people of God.

In writing this book I have very much had in mind people, young and old, who are approaching the Prayer of the Church for the first time, especially those who would like to make it part of their regular prayer-life but fear that it is too complicated. However, it is my hope that what I have written may also help those already committed to the Prayer of the Church, whether they are clerical or lay. It was a priest, renowned for his witticisms, who described the Office as 'a dangerous occasion of prayer'! The burden of this book is that we should gladly surrender to that dangerous occasion; fully aware of its potential, we should be resolved to exploit the Prayer of the Church to the best of our ability. Outside the Mass and the Sacraments, there simply is no other devotion which ranks so highly among the many forms of worship encouraged by the Church.

Because the history of the Prayer of the Church is itself both revealing and encouraging, chapter one ('The Prayer of the Church in the Making') tells the story of how this Prayer came into existence in the first centuries of Christianity, how in those far-off days it was truly 'The People's Office' in that it involved the whole local Church; how later it was highjacked by the monks and later still became privatised and clericalised (it became 'the prayer that Father prays on his own from his little black book'), and finally how in the second half of the twentieth century the Church has sought to restore it to its former glory – and return it to the whole people of God.

Such a restoration would never have been attempted but for the conviction that the Prayer of the Church is a devotion of unique value. Chapter two ('The Importance of the Prayer of the Church') explores some of the reasons that underlie that conviction: the fact that it is the Church community's unceasing prayer in which we are privileged to take part; the fact that it is a supremely trinitarian prayer in which, united with Christ and by the power of the Spirit, we give praise and worship to the Father; the fact that it is liturgical prayer and as such continues Christ's redeeming work in the world; the fact that it is staggered over the course of each twenty-four hours and so helps to dedicate the whole day to the Lord; and the fact that throughout the ages it has functioned as a school of prayer for countless men and women, the world over. However, there is another fact to be added to that list: the fact that the Prayer of the Church is locked into the Church's celebration of the liturgical year, through which the entire mystery of Christ is unfolded year by year, and through which the memory of, and communion with, our sisters and brothers, the saints, are kept alive. It is this aspect of the Prayer of the Church which is tackled in chapter five: 'Seasons and Saints in the Prayer of the Church'.

Even in the two chapters concerned with how the various parts of the Prayer of the Church are to be celebrated – chapters three and six – the emphasis is not so much on 'mechanics' as on how this or that section can become a true celebration, a genuine prayer. Chapter three focuses upon Morning Prayer and Evening Prayer. They are the two key elements of the whole Office and may be as much as many people will be able to manage on a regular basis. However, for those who wish to attempt more, chapter six deals with the other parts of the Prayer of the Church – Prayer during the Day, Night Prayer and Office of Readings. (It may not be inappropriate at this stage to recommend to readers, even those who live busy lives, the praying of Night Prayer, for they will find it a brief but splendid way of ending each day.)

Since the psalms form the backbone of the Prayer of the Church, they deserve, and have received, a chapter to themselves. Anyone seriously desirous of praying the Prayer of the Church must surely devote some time to a consideration of these wonderful songs of praise which have been the prayers of so many people, Jewish and Christian, for the past two to three millenia. A useful introduction to them is to be found in chapter four, 'Psalms in the Prayer of the Church'.

I cannot finish without paying tribute to the Reverend Geoffrey Steel who read this book in manuscript and offered invaluable suggestions. To him belongs the credit for many of the pleasing features of this volume, though he bears no responsibility for any of its defects. I am grateful also to Rosemary Gallagher from Redemptorist Publications for her unfailing words of encouragement, and to my brother Bernard for producing the helpful diagrams.

'Sing to the Lord a new song' is a cry that goes up on several occasions in the psalms. This volume will have achieved its purpose if, by encouraging some newcomers to take up the Prayer of the Church, or by helping some oldhands to rediscover its value, many a 'new song' will be sung joyfully to the Lord.

Note:
References to the **General Instruction on the Liturgy of the Hours** will be abbreviated to "**GI**" and the number of the particular section of the document referred to.

References to the **Constitution on the Liturgy** will be abbreviated to "**CL**" and the number of the particular section of the document referred to.

1 – The Prayer of the Church in the Making

'The Church's praise is not to be considered either by origin or by nature the exclusive possession of clerics and monks but the property of the whole Christian community.' (General Instruction on the Liturgy of the Hours §270)[1]

The Prayer of the Church takes different forms and people are first attracted to it in a variety of ways. They may have been haunted by hearing it chanted in a monastery, or taken part in it themselves during a retreat, or been entranced by the beauty of an English choral service on the radio; or perhaps, as for a person I was speaking to recently, it was excerpts from the psalms heard at Mass which first gave them the desire to take up a prayer in which the psalms play a key role. I still remember with gratitude the day when our parish decided that we would take up the Prayer of the Church, or at any rate its two central parts, Morning and Evening Prayer, each day.

From then onwards, every morning, and again every evening, a little group of us would gather in church for prayer. Of course there were parishioners who simply couldn't be there; they were sick, or they had other important tasks to see to, like getting the children off to school, or going to work, or looking after an aged parent; though it was good to discover that some of them were with us in spirit, for they prayed the Prayer of the Church at home, either with a partner (a husband, for example, or a friend) or on their own. It is fascinating to learn that way back in the Church's history the Bishop of Constantinople St John Chrysostom – he died in 407 – used to advise lay people unable to attend public worship in the morning and evening to pray at the same times wherever they might happen to be.

Most of our parishioners, for whatever reason, were simply not interested, and there were a few who were frankly puzzled by the whole idea. An elderly house-bound invalid fired a couple of no-nonsense questions: 'Where did this new-fangled devotion come from?' he wanted to know;

and 'What's so important about it, anyway?' It seems to me that these are the very questions that might occur to anyone who is thinking of taking up the practice of praying the Prayer of the Church for the first time. That is why the next two chapters will try to offer a satisfactory answer to each of them.

In the first place, then, where did the Prayer of the Church come from? How did it come into being? How did it arrive at its present shape? After all, on Ascension day the Lord did not send out his apostles, each with the Prayer of the Church tucked under his arm. So, where *did* it come from? To that apparently simple question there is no simple answer. The history of the Prayer of the Church (the Office, or the Divine Office, as it is often called), especially its early history, is pretty obscure and often highly complex. There was nothing like uniformity throughout the Church: what happened in York was not necessarily what was happening in Rome, or what happened in Spain the same as was happening in North Africa. Nonetheless, the detective work of scholars – though of course even scholars are not in agreement on every issue – has, in broad outline, brought to light the development of the Prayer of the Church. It is a fascinating story, and not without its lessons for us today.

Back to Roots

There is a sense in which the Prayer of the Church was already being fashioned before ever the Church came into existence. Its roots are to be found deep in the Old Testament; more precisely, in the religious practice of the Jews and above all in the words and example of the Jew par excellence, Jesus Christ. It was in the school of Jewish daily prayer that he learned to pray. The pious Jew would recite morning and evening the 'Shema'. Strictly speaking, the Shema was not so much a prayer as a profession of faith, a creed expressing belief in the absolute oneness of God. Its name comes from the Hebrew word with which it begins and which means 'Hear' or 'Listen'. This is how it runs:

'Hear, O Israel:
The Lord is our God, the Lord alone.
You shall love the Lord your God
with all your heart,
and with all your soul,
and with all your might.
Keep these words that I am commanding you today in your heart.
Recite them to your children
and talk about them
when you are at home and when you are away,
when you lie down and when you rise'
(*Deuteronomy 6:4-7; NRSV*).
(It was the reference to 'lying down' and 'rising' which suggested recitation of these verses in the evening and in the morning.) The Shema itself was preceded and followed by a series of 'blessings', prayers which blessed God by means of praise and thanksgiving.

Another prayer, which came to be linked with the Shema in the morning and evening, was also recited on its own in the afternoon. The book of the prophet Daniel describes how its hero was thrown into the lions' den for disobeying a law which forbade the Jewish people to pray to anyone except the king. However, despite the dreadful penalty that threatened, Daniel, from an upstairs room whose window faced towards Jerusalem, 'three times each day... went down on his knees, praying and giving praise to God as he had always done' (*Daniel 6:10*). The prayer he was reciting three times each day – probably corresponding to the times of the principal acts of worship in the Temple – was the 'Tephilla', which means simply 'prayer' or better, in this context, the prayer. (Interestingly, Tephilla is derived from a Hebrew word which means, literally, 'to judge oneself': prayer results from the acknowledgement of our own smallness and insignificance, our absolute dependence on God.) It consisted of a series of blessings, prayers which all began with the words 'Blessed are You' (rather like the prayers said at Mass when our gifts of bread and wine are placed on the altar in preparation for the eucharistic prayer).

Here is the first of them:
'Blessed are You –
the Lord our God and God of our fathers,
the God of Abraham, God of Isaac, and God of Jacob,
the great, mighty and revered God,
the Most High God, who bestows loving kindness,
the Creator of all things, who remembers the good deeds of the fathers, and in love will bring a redeemer to their children's children for his name's sake[2].'

So we can imagine Jesus at sunrise, before any other activity, again at three o'clock in the afternoon (the hour of sacrifice in the Temple) and once more at nightfall, turning towards Jerusalem and the Temple and praying aloud, with his *tallith* or prayer shawl wrapped about him. Of course there were many other traditional prayers used by the Jews, in addition to the Shema and the Tephilla: there was grace before and after meals, for example, there were the psalms, there was the Sabbath liturgy of the word in the synagogue. Moreover, the Temple was the scene for liturgical ceremonies involving musical instruments of all kinds, singing, dancing, the burning of incense, processions.

O praise him with sound of trumpet,
praise him with lute and harp.
Praise him with timbrel and dance,
praise him with strings and pipes.
O praise him with resounding cymbals
praise him with clashing of cymbals.

You can't hear these words from Psalm 150 without realising that the Jewish people knew how to celebrate. Indeed, I suspect their Temple services would leave our modern services, even the most charismatic of them, looking very tame in comparison.

It was from this prayerful people that Jesus came, so that from the start he was well groomed in the ways of prayer, personal and communal. Indeed the Gospels make it clear that his prayer-life went far beyond what was then the requirement. He prayed early 'in the morning, long before dawn' (*Mark 1:35*); he prayed late at night and sometimes even 'spent the whole night in prayer' (*Luke 6:12*); again, from time to time 'he would go off to some deserted place and pray' (*Luke 5:16*). St Luke tells us how his disciples, not for the first or last time I suspect, found him 'praying alone' (*Luke 9:18*). There were times, however, when he prayed in the presence of others, as at his baptism (*Luke 3:21*) for instance, or at the transfiguration (*Luke 9:29*). He resorted to prayer in times of joy and gratitude (*Luke 10:21*), but also in times of most terrible crisis, as in the garden of Gethsemane (*Mark 14:32f*) and on the Cross (*Matthew 27:46; Luke 23:34*).

There is a fair amount of evidence in the New Testament about the praying of the first Christians, though it leaves many questions – such as the nature of their prayer, the times of prayer – unanswered. On the one hand, since they were Jews it would have been strange indeed had they not continued the practice of praying at the three traditional times of the day; but, on the other hand, since they were also followers of Jesus who presented himself as the incarnation of a new way of approaching God, it would have been surprising had there not been a radical 'newness' in their prayer: new wine required new wineskins. The newness is summed up in the single Aramaic word 'Abba'. It may seem strange that the original word has been kept by the authors of the New Testament – you'll find it in *Mark 14:36*, in *Romans 8:15* and again in *Galatians 4:6* – but could that be because they could not find an exact equivalent? For example, though it might be translated into English as 'dear Father', that does not do it justice. In fact there is no precise English equivalent: it is such an intimate term that it was reserved for use in the immediate family circle. It seems unlikely that the Jews would have dared to use it in addressing God. But there was one Jew who did dare. Jesus used Abba in his prayer; and, when his friends asked him to teach them how to pray, he dared them (and us) to follow his example: 'When you pray, say: "Our Father" (Abba)' (*Matthew 6:9*). The whole purpose of his coming was to redeem us, which is another way of saying that he came to make us his brothers and sisters, to draw us into such close union with himself that we would become adopted members of the divine family circle, and by that very fact entitled to call upon God as Abba. Indeed, the 'Our Father' is the only recorded prayer that Jesus ever taught his followers. St Paul sums up the situation admirably in his letter to the Christians in Galatia (*4:6*) when he writes: 'God has sent into our hearts the Spirit of his Son crying

"Abba, Father" '. One of the earliest Christian writings we have is known as the 'Didache' which some experts date as early as the year 60, before any of the Gospels had been written; in chapter 8 of that book the faithful are enjoined to recite the 'Our Father' three times each day. It is 'the first explicit, unambiguous reference to a system of daily prayer in the primitive Church'[3].

Some of the great Christian writers, such as Clement of Alexandria, Tertullian, Origen and Cyprian, who all lived in the second half of the second century and the first half of the third, seem to have been haunted by our Lord's words that we must 'persevere in prayer and not lose heart' (*Luke 18:1*) and by Paul's insistence that we must 'pray without ceasing' (*1 Thessalonians 5:17*). The true follower of Jesus should pray unceasingly. But they could see that there was little likelihood of that unless Christian people were prepared to set aside some definite times for prayer each day. Even when they observed such prayer-times individually or within the family, they realised that their prayer was corporate rather than individual for they knew that they were united in spirit with other Christians who at about these same times were engaged in similar exercises.

However, it is especially in the book 'Apostolic Tradition', written in Rome by Hippolytus, possibly early in the third century, that evidence begins to appear of a pattern of **daily prayer-times**. From then onwards there are fairly frequent recommendations to pray: on the one hand, in the Christian assembly, in the morning and evening when there would be scripture readings, an instruction, and no doubt the praying of psalms; and, on the other hand, in private at 9 am, at noon and at 3 pm. But that was not all; the faithful were encouraged, though not obliged, to rise for prayer in the middle of the night (mindful of Jesus' parable about the bridegroom who arrived at midnight and found only the wise bridesmaids awaiting him) and, finally, they were urged to greet each new dawn with a service of prayer.

There is no means of knowing how many ordinary Christians would have followed such a demanding prayer regime – five prayer-times during each day, as well as one during the night and another at first light. However, it is worth remembering that there was great religious fervour at this period in the Church's history. To become a Christian at all demanded a high level of commitment; it was almost like entering a religious order nowadays – and a very strict one, at that. Moreover, what seems to us an extreme demand may not have seemed so to them: rising in the middle of the night, for example, might not have been quite so difficult in times when people got to bed as soon as darkness had fallen and so had the prospect of a long night's sleep. In any event it seems that many of the early Christians valued a programme of prayer which enabled them to consecrate the whole day and night to God.

The Formative Period

i) *The 'People's Office'*

At the beginning of the fourth century, the Roman Empire got a new overlord. Emperor Constantine was favourable to Christianity and his accession sparked off events comparable to those witnessed in Eastern Europe after the fall of the Berlin Wall in 1989: peace came to the Church after years of persecution and victimisation. Before long, large churches were being erected and soon Morning and Evening Prayers had become **daily public services**, attended by large numbers of people. At these gatherings the faithful sang 'morning psalms' (especially Psalm 62[4]: 'O God, you are my God, for you I long') and 'evening psalms' (especially 140: 'I have called to you, Lord: hasten to help me!'), selected psalms which did not vary and were known by heart; to them were added intercessions and a final prayer by the leader which was known as a collect. Morning Prayer – consisting of praise and thanksgiving for the new day and for salvation in Christ Jesus – was considered the appropriate way for a Christian to begin and dedicate the new day, just as Evening Prayer – consisting of thanksgiving for the day's graces and a plea both for pardon of the day's faults and for divine protection during the night hours – was considered the appropriate way for a Christian to close it.

Because these public celebrations took place in the bishop's church, they are usually referred to by scholars as the 'cathedral Offices' – a title which distinguishes them from the 'monastic Offices' we shall be hearing about shortly. However, the bishop's church in those days was almost the equivalent of a parish church of today; that is why the prayer services which took place there morning and evening are perhaps better described as the 'People's Offices'. They were a popular form of liturgy, attended by all the members of the local church in a particular area. There would be readers and singers, processions and chants, and, in the evening, the twinkling of oil lamps and billowing clouds of incense. And so we are brought face to face with a striking and challenging fact: originally, the Prayer of the Church was precisely that – not the special preserve of the clergy but the Prayer of the whole People of God. And just as the prayer of the people was not 'borrowed' from the clergy, neither was it borrowed from the monks, because, almost certainly, the 'monastic Offices' were a later arrival.

ii) *The 'Monastic Offices*

From earliest times there were men and women who felt called to consecrate their lives to God through practices of severe discipline and prolonged prayer. Some, at least initially, lived in their own homes and joined other Christians in the local church for public worship (the 'urban' monks, as they are called), while others withdrew into the wilderness (the 'desert' monks). The latter, represented especially by the monks of the Egyptian desert, seem to have had only two services each day – one at the beginning, the other at the end; furthermore, they were not so much liturgical services as occasions for communal meditation on the psalms. Moreover, the monks in this tradition sought to observe as literally as possible the precept of ceaseless prayer by the constant use of all 150 psalms in strict rotation. There were even some groups which made sure that the praying of the psalter would continue non-stop, by organising themselves into a kind of shift system, thereby ensuring that there would be no time of day or night when the psalms were not being prayed. Such groups were to be found in some of the ancient monasteries of Ireland and Wales, such as that at Bangor. (It was this practice of unceasing praying of the psalms which gave rise to what became known as monasteries of 'sleepless ones', and at a later time to convents of 'perpetual adoration'.)

The urban monks also recited the whole psalter in rotation but only once per week, rather than non-stop by day and night. They joined in Morning and Evening Prayer, as we have seen, but in addition they continued to follow those other five 'Hours' of prayer that had been recommended in earlier days – at the third, sixth and ninth hours, during the night and at cockcrow. As if that were not enough, some of them introduced a new bed-time Office which consisted of Psalm 90 ('He who dwells in the shelter of the Most High') followed by prayers; it was soon in almost universal use and became known as Completorium (Compline), because it 'completed' the day's prayer. Finally, towards the end of the fourth century it seems that the monks of Bethlehem were responsible for the introduction of yet another time of prayer, called the 'first Hour' or Prime. (Apparently, its initial purpose was to discourage lazy monks from returning to bed after prayer at dawn and remaining there until the next Hour at nine o'clock!)

At this stage, the shape of the Prayer of the Church, at least the shape familiar in the west until the time of the Second Vatican Council in the early 1960s, had been achieved. It consisted of seven 'Hours', or times, of prayer during each day and one 'Hour' during the night. They were as follows:

Lauds (morning)
Prime (first Hour)
Terce (third Hour)
Sext (sixth Hour)
None (ninth Hour)
Vespers (evening)
Compline (end of day), and the
night Hour of Mattins[5] (also known as Nocturns or Vigils)

Morning Prayer, because it is predominantly a time of praise, was known as Lauds (from the latin Laudes = praises), Evening Prayer as Vespers (from the latin Vespera = evening), while the Hours at the third, sixth and ninth hours[6] were called 'Terce', 'Sext' and 'None', respectively.

The arrangement of seven Hours by day and one by night may have been influenced by the words of Psalm 118, verse 164: '<u>Seven times</u> a day I praise you' and verse 147: 'I rise before dawn and call for your help'. From at least the third century the various Hours of the Office were given a spiritual significance by being linked with key events in the history of the early Church, such as the coming of the Holy Spirit at the third Hour (*Acts 2:15*). Soon, however, they were linked even more firmly to stages in the Passion of Christ, a practice which continued into the Middle Ages, when 'Hours of the Passion', based upon the sequence of the Hours of the Office, were fairly common[7]. Here, for example, is a hymn written by an anonymous medieval author, using slight variations in the names of some of the Hours given above:

At *Mattins* bound,
At *Prime* reviled,
Condemned to death at *Tierce*,
Nailed to the Cross at *Sexts*,
at *Nones* His blessed side they pierce.
They take him down at *Vesper*-tide,
In grave at *Compline* lay:
Who thenceforth bids His Church observe
the sevenfold hours alway.

iii) *The People's Office Disappears*

Not surprisingly, most people could not get to all the Offices each day and on the whole were content to attend Morning and Evening Prayer. For a considerable time – longer in the eastern part of the Church than in the western – the People's Office and the Monastic Office ran side by side. But from about the sixth century there was a merging of the two. It might be more accurate to say that there was a take-over of the one by the other: little by little the People's Office was supplanted by the Monastic Office. The former became less and less the prayer of the whole People of God, as it had been from the start, and more and more the specialised prayer of monks, clergy and religious[8], with its seven Hours of prayer by day and one by night, and with its incorporation of all 150 psalms into each week's Office. In the West it was Saint Benedict (c.480-550) more than anyone who gave the Office the broad outline it has retained until recent times; it was he who spoke of it as 'the work of God' (Opus Dei); and it was monks, such as Bede, Benedict Biscop and Augustine of Canterbury, Chad and

Aidan – men reflecting Benedictine spirituality – who brought it to England in the sixth century and beyond. Bede, who 'may well be reckoned the most truly educated and attractive man to be found anywhere in his day'[9], was reputed to know all 150 psalms by heart and sang parts of the Office of the day as he lay dying.

However, not only was the Office 'monasticised' (tailor-made to suit monks), it was also 'privatised' (reduced to a form suitable for individual recitation – obviously the last thing that the Prayer of the Church was meant to be). In earlier centuries the Christian population of the towns had been small and the number of clergy fairly large, so that clerics, together with their bishop, had no difficulty in chanting the daily Offices in common. But Christians continued to increase in numbers and by about the middle of the twelfth century each locality was left with just one priest in charge; this was particularly the case in northern Europe where dioceses were huge in comparison with those of Italy. Clearly, it was no longer possible for a parish priest to celebrate the whole of the Office publicly in church each day as well as attending to the many pastoral tasks waiting to be done. Various solutions were attempted, such as reciting the different Hours in rota fashion, one Hour in one church, another Hour in another, and so on. But eventually, and sadly, a move was made from the public to the private celebration of the Prayer of the Church, a practice which was made possible by the appearance of the 'breviary'.

The Breviary

In earlier times the Office, made up almost entirely of the psalms, was known by heart by monks and clergy, but as it became more elaborate the help of books was called for. It has been estimated that as many as ten weighty tomes (such as the Bible, a hymnal, the lectionary, the book of psalms, etc) might be needed for the celebration of one Hour of the Office; sometimes they would be placed on a large lectern which had a revolving top so that the different books could be brought into play, as and when required. The monks would gather round and sing – and the people (of God) would listen to them from afar: the Prayer of the Church was slipping further and further away from the men and women who make up the greater part of the Church. The 'breviary' was created so that the monks could reduce ('abbreviate') the total number of liturgical books required, by gathering them together in a few volumes.

Such books, intended for monastic communities, were of course still far too unwieldy and costly for personal use. Eventually, in the pontificate of Innocent III (1198-1216), smaller portable breviaries began to appear, making it feasible for an individual monk, who was unavoidably absent form his monastery, to recite the Office on his own. Two factors in the thirteenth century contributed to the still more widespread use of the portable breviary. First, the Franciscan Friars, new-style monks who seldom had a stable abode as they swept across Europe in their apostolic tours; they resorted to the use of a breviary so that they could pray their Office wherever they happened to be. Second, the large number of clerical students in the medieval universities who faced the dilemma of either attending lectures or of fulfiling their obligation of praying the Divine Office; they too found an answer to their dilemma in the portable breviary. Eventually the practice of using a breviary spread to the parish clergy, too. And so what do we find? What had initially been the choral and communal prayer of the whole Christian community, clergy and laity alike, had now become the individual and personal obligation of priests and monks.

The Second Vatican Council (1962-65)

General Councils bring together, in principle, all the bishops of the Church and are rare events: there has been only a score of them in the past two thousand years. The most recent, the Second Vatican Council (often referred to as Vatican II), must rank as one of the most important – and most unexpected. In 1958 a new Pope was elected; at the age of 77, John XXIII was widely regarded as a caretaker pope, but within three months he took the world by surprise when, in January 1959, he announced his intention of calling the twenty-first General Council; he defined its immediate task as that of of renewing the religious life of the Church and bringing up to date in accordance with the needs of the time its teaching, discipline and organisation, with the ultimate goal of unity among all Christians.

Attended by some two and half thousand bishops from every corner of the world, the Council lasted for over three years. However, in its earliest session it was agreed that the first topic to be tackled should be the liturgy, 'the Church with her face turned towards God', as it has been beautifully described. Pope Paul VI, John XXIII's successor, noted that 'the liturgy was the first subject to be examined (in the Council), and,' he added, 'first too, in a sense, in intrinsic worth and in importance for the life of the Church.' For of course our public worship – and that is what liturgy means – is at the core of the Christian life. It was on 4 December 1963 that the Council's document on the liturgy was formally approved[10]. It set the tone for all subsequent sessions of the Council. Its fourth chapter is devoted to the Divine Office, which it pictures as the voice of the Bride (the Church) addressing the Bridegroom (Christ): 'All who take part in the divine office,' it declares, 'are ... sharing in what is the greatest honour for Christ's Bride; for by offering these praises to God they are standing before God's throne in the name of the Church' (*§85*).

In the decades preceding the Council there had been many calls for a revision of the breviary, but no consensus as to what needed to be done. At least three main approaches seem to have been advocated. The first held that the richness of tradition should not be lost – the Office should remain basically as it was; the second argued that though the Office might be admirable for contemplative monks and nuns, it scarcely met the needs of busy priests and religious, let alone harassed housewives and other 'secular' workers, and so needed to be simplified in some way; and the third, initially a small voice raised especially among bishops from the Eastern Catholic churches[11], urged that an attempt be made to ensure that the Office could once again become the Prayer of the whole Church, as indeed it had always been in the East. The chapter of the Constitution reflects to some extent all three approaches, as does the completely revised Divine Office, which was called for by the Council and was finally promulgated by Paul VI in 1970.

In the first place, it retains the traditional use of the psalms and of Scripture in general; indeed one of the most striking features of the revised Office is that it provides such a generous offering of Scripture readings. Furthermore, the Office has been so structured that, as the Constitution on the Sacred Liturgy puts it, 'in keeping with ancient Christian tradition... the whole course of the day and night is consecrated by the praise of God...' (*§84*). Indeed its official, though not exclusive, title is now *The Liturgy of the Hours*, suggesting that this is a way in which we may respond to the New Testament injunction to 'pray always', and by so doing sanctify the various parts of the day and all its various activities.

Secondly, the Office has been streamlined to make it less burdensome to clergy with pastoral responsibilities and at the same time more within the bounds of possibility for the laity. Thus, the number of hours has been reduced from eight to five, and at the same time Morning and Evening Prayer, which since earliest times featured as the common prayer of all the faithful, are highlighted as the most important hours of all, 'the two hinges on which the daily office turns' (*Constitution on the Sacred Liturgy §89*). The psalter continues to be recited virtually in its entirety, but now not every week, as in the past, but every month; intercessions have been added, prayers have been revised and, as already mentioned, a much richer assortment of Scripture readings included. The Office has also been translated into the vernacular and so has become more readily accessible. Many are disappointed at the absence of inclusive language in the Prayer of the Church, particularly in the intercessions where the frequent appearance of all male language tends to jar on the ear. However, the situation can easily be remedied by changing 'brothers' to 'brothers and sisters', 'all men' to 'all men and women' or simply 'all'.

Thirdly, and perhaps most important of all, the Office has been restored as the Prayer of the Church. In his Apostolic Constitution, *Laudis Canticum*, which promulgated the revised breviary, Paul VI summarised the history sketched in this chapter and went on to insist that the first aim of the renewal was to ensure that the Divine Office should once again become the prayer of the <u>whole</u> Church, and not simply that of clergy and religious. 'The Office,' he explained, 'has been ... arranged in such a way that not only clergy but also religious and indeed the laity may participate in it, since it is the prayer of the whole people of God.'

The General Instruction on the Liturgy of the Hours

Time alone will tell whether the revision has gone far enough, especially where the laity are concerned, and to what extent, therefore, it will achieve its purpose. Doubts have been expressed, suggesting that the revision has fallen between several stools, that it is still too complicated, still too monastic, that a much more radical overhaul is called for. That may be so, but few who prayed the Office in pre-Vatican II days would question that it represents a marked improvement on what was once available. More important still, despite the shortcomings of the Prayer of the Church, a growing number of lay people seem to be drawn to the praying of the Hours and to be finding it of great help in their spiritual journey.

A further point must be made: the revision of the breviary was the occasion for the publication of one of the most valuable official documents ever produced on the Prayer of the Church. Its full title is 'The General Instruction on the Liturgy of the Hours'; it was published in 1971, as part of the new breviary, and falls into five chapters, dealing with:

first, the importance of the Liturgy of the Hours in the life of the Church;
second, the various Hours that make up the Office;
third, the various parts that make up the Hours;
fourth, the various celebrations that make up the liturgical year;
fifth, the various tasks and rites involved in communal celebration[12].

Since, as you might expect, the Instruction will often be quoted in the coming pages, it will be useful to abbreviate it as 'GI' and add the number of the particular section of the document referred to; similarly, 'CL' will be used as an abbreviation for the Constitution on the Liturgy. The first quotation I would like to offer is one which makes it clear that the last word has not yet been spoken on the revision of the breviary:

> 'The Liturgy of the Hours is then not seen as a beautiful memorial of the past, demanding intact preservation as an object of admiration; rather it is seen as open to constantly new forms of life and growth and to being the unmistakable sign of a community's vibrant vitality... There is also great hope that new ways and expressions of public worship may be found for our own age, as has clearly always happened in the life of the Church' (*GI§273*).

In this first chapter, as we have followed the story of the making of the Prayer of the Church, we have also discovered at least two reasons why we are justified in calling it 'the Prayer of the People of God'. The first is that in one form or another it is virtually as old as the Church; it has always belonged to us, so that, far from being a new-fangled devotion, its deepest roots go back to the Lord who by word and example taught us to pray. The second is because, as Paul VI has insisted, one of the main purposes of the revision was to ensure that the Office should once again become the prayer of 'the whole People of God', which of course is what it was at its inception. In fact, the reason why 'the Church commissions (the clergy) to celebrate the liturgy of the hours' is, we are told, 'to ensure at least in their persons the regular carrying out of the duty of the whole community ...' (*GI§28; underlining added*).

However, there is yet another reason for describing the Office as the 'Prayer of the People of God'. It emerges from all that has been said so far, even if it has not been explicitly mentioned: that the essence of the Church is that it is a community and it is 'in prayer (that it) must express itself as a community' (*GI§9*). This is borne out by the first glimpse we catch of the infant Church in the pages of the New Testament: the community of the faithful gathered together in prayer with the apostles and Mary the Mother of Jesus (*Acts 1:14*). From the beginning those who had been baptised 'remained faithful to the teaching of the apostles, to the brotherhood, to the breaking of bread and to the prayers' (*Acts 2:42;* emphasis added), no doubt remembering our Lord's own promise: 'Where two or three meet in my name, I am there among them' (*Matthew 18:20*). But apart from that wonderful promise, it is natural that Christians should feel the need to pray with their brothers and sisters, as well as on their own, and that therefore they should design some kind of structured prayer in which they can all participate. As the Vatican Council explains, God 'has ... willed to make women and men holy and to save them, not as individuals without any bond between them, but rather to make them into a people' (*Constitution on the Church §9*); and so it seems inevitable that Christians, not simply as individuals but also as a people, should raise their voices together in prayer and praise to God. Is not that the reason why all the major Christian Churches – Roman Catholic, Anglican, Orthodox, Lutheran, etc – have some form of communal prayer, a daily Office of some kind? (And, incidentally, how grateful we should be to our Anglican and Protestant brothers and sisters who have kept the Prayer of the Church alive through recent centuries by their daily services of Mattins and Evensong.)

In chapter two we must try and answer the second of the two questions posed by the parishioner referred to earlier, namely, how much importance is to be attached to the Divine Office, anyway? Granted that it was originally intended as the common prayer of all God's people, granted too that it has now been revised in a way that makes it more user-friendly, is there any value in this particular prayer, as opposed to any other of the prayers sanctioned by the Church, say, the Rosary or the Stations of the Cross or Novena services?

The first heading of the General Instruction is a brief preview of what answer we might expect: 'The Importance of the Liturgy of the Hours or the Divine Office in the Life of the Church'.

References

1. For further information on this Instruction see below, p22ff

2. Taken from *The Authorised Daily Prayer Book of the United Hebrew Congregations of the Commonwealth* (1990), –p76.

3. Robert Taft SJ in the standard work *The Liturgy of the Hours in East and West,* The Liturgical Press, Collegeville, Minnesota, p13.

4. There are two slightly different ways of numbering the psalms; one follows the Hebrew text, the other the Greek version of the second century BC. The Hebrew numeration is generally one ahead of the Greek, so that 'The Lord is my Shepherd' appears as Psalm 23 in the former but Psalm 22 in the latter. While most modern bibles use the Hebrew numbering, Catholic and Orthodox liturgical books, including the Prayer of the Church, follow the Greek; it is that numbering which is used throughout this book.

5. Though 'Matins' (or 'Mattins') looks as though it should refer to a morning office (as it does among Anglicans and other Christians), it is in fact the traditional word for a night office, the Office of Readings (an Hour consisting of psalms and extensive readings from Scripture and the writings of spiritual authors). Matins and Lauds were often recited one after the other, so that the two (Matins-and-Lauds) came to be regarded a single Hour.

6. In the ancient world it was customary for the twelve hours of the day (6am to 6pm) to be divided into four three-hour groupings, the first, third, sixth and ninth 'hours'; thus, the third hour = between 9am and noon.

7. R T Davies *Medieval English Lyrics*, Faber & Faber, London (1963), p327.

8. Like monks, 'religious' are Christians (women or men) who take vows of poverty, celibacy and obedience, and commit themselves to live in community. However, unlike monks who are in principle 'cut off' from the world in their monastery, religious engage in every kind of active apostolate, such as nursing, the apostolate of the media, running parishes.

9. D Edwards *Christian England,* Fount Paperbacks, London (1982) Vol 1, p42. Alfred (+890), the great Christian king, had a copy of the book of psalms continually in his possession and is reputed to have been working on a complete Psalter in English when he died (*ibid* p88). In the twelfth century, St Godric from Norfolk, a pedlar, sailor and later hermit, attended the classroom with children at Durham in order to be able to read the psalms (*ibid* p160).

10. See *The Basic Sixteen Documents: Vatican Council II,* ed A Flannery OP, Costello Publishing Co., New York (1996), p117ff.

11. From early times there was a rift between Christians in Western Europe and those in Eastern Europe and Africa. With faults and misunderstandings on both sides, the rift eventually became a 'separation' (schism) between the RC Church and the Eastern Orthodox Churches. The 'Eastern bishops' who attended Vatican II represented the 10 million Eastern Catholics, who have retained (or regained) full communion with Rome. (Sometimes they are referred to as 'Uniates', but the word can have a pejorative sense.) Eastern Catholics – to be found, for example, in Greece, the Balkans, Russia, Romania, Poland, Syria, as well as among immigrants in the United States and in the UK – have generally maintained their original traditions and practices, including a legitimate variety in theological expression of doctrine and, of particular importance in this book, their traditional liturgy.

12. If you have access to the three-volumed edition of the breviary, you will find the Instruction in full at the beginning of volume one. Quotations from the instruction given in this book are all taken from the translation in *'Documents on the Liturgy 1963-1979'* The Liturgical Press, Collegeville, Minnesota (1986).

2 – The Importance of the Prayer of the Church

'...the Church's School of Prayer' R Taft SJ[1]

'There was something about the regular saying of the daily offices that entered into your whole being. You might not be aware of every individual word but you were slowly taking it all in and digesting it until it became part of you and your life' [2].

In days gone by, when the Prayer of the Church was thought to be of no concern to the laity, and when many of the clergy regarded it more as a burden than a blessing, a task to be achieved with ruthless adherence to the rules, two priests were travelling along a country road late at night. A glance at their watches told them that it was now almost midnight, the deadline for completing the Office of that day. At once the car slowed to a halt, disgorging its two passengers, who immediately sank to their knees in front of the bonnet. There, in the glare of the headlights, they began reading their breviary. Just then a huge lorry came rumbling by; its driver was scarcely able to believe his eyes. 'Blimey, Jimmie,' he called to his mate, 'just look at that. All I can say is: it must be a ruddy good book!' He was nearer the truth than he realised.

That book, or at any rate the prayer to which it invites us, holds a unique place in the life of the Church. Today, when the Prayer of the Church admits of much greater flexibility than it did in the past and when the laity are once more being encouraged to make it their prayer, too, it is appropriate to ask: why does the Church regard this particular form of prayer so highly, indeed as her daily prayer par excellence? Many reasons might be given; to some extent they overlap but it will perhaps be useful to take them one by one and examine them in some detail. So, here they are:

Never on Your Own

What's so special about this particular prayer? First, the fact that it is the prayer of the Church.

'You'll never walk alone!' is a song which, in no small measure, owes its popularity, especially among those who fight for justice, to the fact that its words and music galvanise people for a common cause, uplift them, give them a powerful sense of solidarity with one another; theirs is not the lonely, hopeless struggle it may seem to be.

The very title 'Prayer of the Church' makes it clear that when we pray the Divine Office, we never pray alone, we are supported and upheld by others; our efforts are caught up in an immense chorus of prayer that ascends to God from the four corners of the globe throughout the whole twenty-four hours of the day – as it has been doing for almost twenty centuries. Each time we open the breviary for prayer we are linked with a host of people beyond counting who raise their voices in praise of God. The idea is well expressed in John Ellerton's hymn, 'The day thou gavest, Lord, is ended', which has its place among the night-time hymns in the Prayer of the Church:

'We thank thee that thy Church unsleeping
While earth rolls onward into light,
Through all the world her watch is keeping,
And rests not now by day or night

As over continent and island
The dawn leads on another day,
The voice of prayer is never silent,
Nor dies the strain of praise away.

The sun that bids us rest is waking
Our brethren 'neath the western sky,
And hour by hour fresh lips are making
Thy wondrous doings heard on high.'

Indeed, CL has a vision of the Divine Office which is not merely universal but cosmic; it sees it encompassing the men and women of this world, but also those of the next; for Jesus, our great High Priest, has 'introduced into this earthly exile that hymn which is sung in the realms above' (CL§83). Thus, in praying the Office 'we take part in a foretaste of that heavenly liturgy which is celebrated in the holy city of Jerusalem toward which we journey as pilgrims' (CL§8). Of course the praying of the Prayer of the Church cannot always be a profound religious experience: we shall be distracted, disappointed, disheartened at times; but, as has been wisely and encouragingly said, 'What matters is that we should be, slowly and quietly, moulded by this rehearsal for and anticipation of the worship of heaven. It is a schooling for paradise'3.

Because it is the Prayer of the Church, it should of course be prayed aloud – indeed, most of it should be sung – by the whole Christian community, the Church made visible in this or that particular locality. Yet even when it is prayed alone and in silence by an individual, it does not cease to be **public** prayer, prayer in the name of, and on behalf of, the whole Church, prayer in union with all those who at this time are praying that same prayer. The fact that we are not alone means that our efforts, however puny, still have value, for they are part of a much wider, much richer, God-inspired symphony that never ceases. We might be compared to rather indifferent singers who would not dream of performing solo before a large audience, yet are more than happy to be part of a chorus; in such reassuring company we find to our joy that we are contributing to a sound more splendid by far than anything we could have imagined, let alone have accomplished on our own.

However, if communal prayer has a special value and richness, it can also appear to have an unfortunate draw-back: communal prayer is usually structured, and structured prayer cannot suit all the people all the time; nor is it intended to do so. There will inevitably be occasions when a psalm does not speak to me; it has no obvious bearing upon my particular mood or upon any of my current needs or concerns; it may even run counter to them. How, for example, am I to pray a psalm brimming with threats and cries for vengeance when I am feeling full of goodwill towards the whole human race? On the other hand, how am I to make my own a psalm which rejoices over the goodness and utter faithfulness of God when at this moment I am feeling decidedly annoyed because of how he seems to have let me down?

I believe that one of the beauties of the Office is that it encourages us to be unselfish in our prayer, not to be enslaved by personal feelings but liberated enough to look to the needs of others. There is no psalm, however dark or threatening, that does not express the sentiments of some person or group of people; why then can we not pray it in their name? We live in a world where atrocious things happen – boys and girls apprenticed to prostitution from childhood, people tortured for their beliefs, maimings and killings perpetrated in the name of religion – and one of the strengths of the psalms is that they enable us, if we will, to live in this real world where bad as well as good things happen. A few years ago a woman who had been imprisoned for thirteen months in Indonesia was being interviewed on radio. She had never had to face physical torture herself, she explained – though many of her companions had – but she had lived with the fear of torture hanging over her for weeks on end. Conditions were just about as grim as they could be. She was not, as she put it, a 'religious' person, but in her misery found the words of a psalm coming back to mind, a psalm which she had learned long ago at Sunday School. She repeated them now, over and over again, and found that they brought her confidence and hope. The psalm turned out to be Psalm 142, 'Lord, listen to my prayer', (it is used at Night Prayer in the Prayer of the Church every Tuesday night) which is the anguished cry of someone who suffers grievously at the hands of an enemy, who is crushed to the ground, who dwells in darkness and yet who stretches out arms towards God, thirsting for him 'like a (piece of) parched land'. As the woman told her story, the psalm seemed to come to life and I have found ever since that it is hard to recite Psalm 142 without thinking and praying on behalf of anonymous brothers or sisters of mine who are suffering in various parts of the world.

John XXIII, 'Good Pope John' as he was affectionately known, used to devote the various parts of the daily Office to the different parts of the world in which he had served as a priest – France, Turkey, Greece, Bulgaria – remembering the living and the dead of each region in turn; he sensed that the needs of these people beyond his home country of

Italy were all being expressed in the various psalms he prayed in their name. In similar fashion, parents might pray the Office for their children, teachers for the youngsters in their classes, a priest for the families in an area of the parish and so on. At one time, as principal Catholic prison chaplain, I usually had to pray the Prayer of the Church on my own. The only way I could make sense of the situation was to recognise that I was acting as the spokesman before God of tens of thousands of men, women and youngsters in prisons up and down the country, of their spouses and children, of prison officers and staff, of my brother and sister chaplains.

The GI makes it clear that in the Prayer of the Church our horizons stretch out to the ends of the earth: applying to all who pray the Office what the Vatican Council says in particular of priests (in its *Decree on the Ministry and Life of Priests* §5), the Instruction notes that 'they share the ... responsibility of praying to God on behalf of all the people entrusted to them and indeed for the whole world' (*§28, emphasis added*).

Prayer that is Trinitarian

What's so special about this particular prayer? Secondly, the fact that it is the prayer of Christ in the Spirit to The Father.

The Church is often called 'the Sacrament of Christ', the sign and symbol of his presence, and, more than that, the very means by which that presence is continued among us; in the words of a famous theologian: 'As the body is animated by the soul and makes it visible and expresses it ... so the Church is animated by Christ, makes him visible and expresses him'[4]. Perhaps, similarly, the Prayer of the Church might be described as the Sacrament of the Prayer of Christ, one of the chief means by which his prayer endures till the end of time in our midst in the Church. As we saw in the first chapter, one of the most striking features of Jesus' life was his devotedness to prayer; prayer at once inspired, and was inspired by, all that he did; without it, his life would be emptied of its deepest meaning.

Nor did he pray only on his own: regularly he took part in the public prayer of the synagogue, as well as the worship of the Temple in Jerusalem. His praying has not ceased; not only because he continues to intercede for us in heaven (*cf Hebrews 7:25*), but also because 'through his church ... he continues (his) priestly work. The church, by celebrating the Eucharist and in other ways, especially the celebration of the divine office, is ceaselessly engaged in praising the Lord and interceding for the salvation of the entire world' (*CL§83, emphasis added*). The Constitution goes on to say that the official prayer of the Church is 'the prayer which Christ himself together with his Body addresses to the Father' (*§84*). It was mentioned earlier that we never pray alone. That is true, but in an even more breath-taking sense than we may have realised. We never pray alone because our prayer is united with that of our brothers and sisters on earth and in heaven, and, still more remarkably, because it is united with that of Christ. And so as Church it is our privilege not simply to pray with our fellow Christians today, and with countless other Christians down the ages, but also in some wondrous way to find ourselves praying a prayer which engages Christ himself.

St Augustine, who died in 430, never tired of speaking of this intimate union between Christ and Christians, between the Head and the Body, during time of prayer. The GI cannot resist quoting at length from one of his most famous commentaries on the psalms, in which he says:

> 'God could give us no greater gift than to establish as our Head the Word through whom he created all things and to unite us to that Head as members ... The Head is ... one as God with the Father and one as man with us. When we speak in prayer to the Father, we do not separate the Son from him and when the Son's Body prays it does not separate itself from its Head. It is ... the Lord Christ Jesus who prays for us and in us and is prayed to by us. He prays for us as our priest, in us as our head; he is prayed to by us as our God. Recognise therefore our own voice in him and his voice in us' (*§7; emphasis added*).

To express the intimate union between Christ and his Church, especially at prayer, the New Testament uses another image, besides that of the head and the body. It is that of the bridegroom and the bride, an image which appears first in the Old Testament where Israel, God's own people, are so loved by him that he is able to call them his bride. The same symbol is taken up in the New Testament: a bridal or marriage union of even greater intimacy exists between Christ and his Church. And so it is not surprising that one of the traditional ways of referring to the Office has been as 'the voice of the bride'. The CL combines both images: the praying of the Prayer of the Church, it notes, 'is truly the voice of the bride herself addressed to her bridegroom. And what is more, it is the prayer which Christ himself together with his body addresses to the Father'(*§84*).

However there can be no Christian prayer without the Holy Spirit, and so the Prayer of the Church is not only the prayer of Christ, but the prayer of the Holy Spirit, or, to put it another way, the Church prays to the Father both through Christ and in the Holy Spirit for it is through Christ that we 'have access in one spirit to the Father' (*Ephesians 2:18*). 'The unity of the Church at prayer is brought about by the Holy Spirit, the ... Spirit who is the same in Christ, in the whole Church, and in every baptised person' (*GI§8*). St Paul expresses this powerfully when he says that the Spirit is actively involved in our praying, actually voicing more than we could ever find words for, thereby ensuring that the prayers 'of the saints' (Paul's way of referring to the baptised) are acceptable to the Father (*see Romans 8:26-27*). Mgr James Crichton, the doyen of English liturgists, goes so far as to say that the Office, 'however formal in appearance, is the supreme charismatic prayer of the Church in which we can be sure that the Holy Spirit is present and active'[5].

The Prayer of the Church, then, does indeed draw us into a most magnificent company – not only that of all our Christian brothers and sisters, on earth and in heaven, not only that of Jesus, but that of the most Holy Trinity.

A fourteenth-century picture, called 'The Trinity', is to be found in a psalter from Engelberg in Switzerland; this suggests that the notion of linking the psalms with the Trinity is no recent discovery. In praying the Prayer of the

Church, we are immersed in a sublime task: through the Spirit we are being caught up into Christ's own prayer to the Father. It is an encouraging, bewildering, almost incredible thought; yet it is a truth that we are reminded of countless times in the Prayer of the Church, for every psalm is brought to a close with: 'Glory be to the Father, and to the Son, and to the Holy Spirit'.

Christ's Redemptive Work Continued

What's so special about this particular prayer? Thirdly, the fact that it is liturgical prayer.

Like science or any other discipline, spirituality has its own technical terms and one of them is 'liturgy'. It comes from two Greek words, meaning, respectively, 'people' (*laos*) and 'work' (*ergon*). In ancient Greece liturgy had a secular connotation: it referred to a public work, something done for the good of the people, of the community; thus, paying taxes was a form of 'liturgising'! However, that usage has long since disappeared and nowadays 'liturgy' refers to the work of the people (of God), or, as Pius XII described it, 'the public worship which our Redeemer ... offers to the heavenly Father and which the community of Christ's faithful pays to its Founder and through him to the Eternal Father'[6]. Since, as we have seen, the Divine Office is the official Prayer of the Church, the People of God, and the prayer of Christ himself, then it obviously qualifies as liturgical prayer; and that means that, together with the Mass and the sacraments, it is one of the basic elements which have nourished the inner life of the Church down the centuries. It ought not to be seen as the poor relation, either, the cinderella among the three; it is neither a second-class nor an optional activity of the Church, but something vital.

The CL instructs us that in the liturgy – and that includes the Prayer of the Church – 'God is perfectly glorified and men and women are sanctified', and that 'every liturgical celebration, because it is an action of Christ the priest and of his body, which is the Church, is a preeminently sacred action' (*§7*). The liturgy is unrivalled in the sense that no other action is so closely related to that of Christ or so powerfully productive of grace. The GI takes this further in an incredible passage in which it explains that 'In the Holy Spirit Christ carries out through the Church "the task of redeeming humanity and giving perfect glory to God", not only when the Eucharist is celebrated and the sacraments administered, but also in other ways, and especially when the liturgy of the hours is celebrated' (*§13, emphasis added*). That really is something: we are being assured that whenever we prayerfully recite the Office – no matter what the circumstances, no matter what our own feelings – Christ is by that very fact continuing his redemptive work in the world. Little wonder that we are told that 'those ... who take part in the Liturgy of the Hours bring growth to God's people in a hidden but fruitful apostolate', that 'the readings and prayers of the Liturgy of the Hours form a wellspring of the Christian life', that it is both the source and the culmination of pastoral and apostolic activity (*§18*), and that 'through public worship and prayer (we) reach all humanity and can contribute significantly to the salvation of the whole world' (*§27*).

The Eucharist is of course the high point of the liturgy, its most sacred action. However, as Paul VI makes clear, there is a very special relationship between the Mass and the Prayer of the Church: he notes how in the history of the Church the Office came to be 'seen as a kind of necessary complement to the fullness of divine worship that is contained in the eucharistic sacrifice, by means of which that worship might overflow to reach all the hours of daily life'. The GI takes up the same theme, showing how on the one hand the Office 'extends to the different hours of the day the praise and thanksgiving, the memorial of the mysteries of salvation ... and the foretaste of heavenly glory that are present in the eucharistic mystery' and on the other 'is in turn an excellent preparation for the celebration of the Eucharist itself' (*§12*). Since Vatican II we have become used to hearing the Eucharist spoken of as the 'source and summit' of the Church's life and mission. Each of those words, 'source' and 'summit', implies both a movement from and a movement towards: a stream bubbles forth *from* its source and moves *towards* the surrounding countryside to bring it freshness and nourishment; similarly, a hill's summit is marked by paths which not only lead up *towards* it but also lead down *from* it to the valley below. Neither the source nor the summit stands on its own, divorced from everything around it; nor is the eucharist cut off from the rest of our daily life. The Prayer of the Church is one of the surest ways of prolonging it throughout the day so that, source-like, its streams of grace may touch and enhance all that we do; at the same time it is an excellent way of preparing ourselves for the next celebration in which we are to be involved, for it arouses the faith and hope and love, and the spirit of praise, which a fruitful celebration of the Eucharist demands. Thus, it helps to ensure that the Mass does not assume the appearance of a lonely, isolated peak; on the contrary, it has paths leading to and from it which enrich our daily lives. That is why the Catechism of the Catholic Church does not hesitate to say that 'the Liturgy of the Hours ... is like an extension of the Eucharistic celebration'[7].

The essence of the Eucharist is that it is a memorial sacrifice, the re-presentation of Jesus' sacrifice on calvary. Clearly, there can be no question of the Divine Office being a sacrifice in that sense. However, the word 'sacrifice' is also used in a much wider fashion in the New Testament – St Paul, for example, speaks of evangelisation as a sacrifice (*Romans 1:9*) and St Peter reminds Christians that they are 'a holy priesthood' called 'to offer the spiritual sacrifices made acceptable to God through Jesus Christ' (*1 Peter 2:5*). The Vatican Council, in its Constitution on the Church, recalls that 'all their (i.e. the laity's) work, if accomplished in the Spirit, become spiritual sacrifices... : their prayer and apostolic undertakings, family and married life, daily work, relaxation ...'(*§34*). However, while these ordinary activities of daily life become 'sacrificial' provided that they are done for the glory of God (and of course they may not be), the unique feature of the Prayer of the Church is that the glory of God is its immediate purpose (not an additional purpose added to it, as in the case of other activities); it is of its nature a sacred activity, it is really, albeit in a broad sense of the word, a sacrifice.

Finally, the fact that the Prayer of the Church is liturgical prayer is the reason it calls for communal celebration. Many of us have become so used to thinking of the Office as a private prayer, the prayer of an individual, the prayer of the priest, that the GI finds it necessary to remind us that though clergy and religious have a 'special mandate' in this matter, yet 'the Church's praise is (not) to be considered by origin (see the last chapter) or by nature (see above in this chapter), the exclusive possession of clerics and monks, but the property of the whole Christian community' (*§270*). Indeed, in an earlier section the Instruction had already made it clear that the laity are positively encouraged 'to fulfil the Church's duty by celebrating (at least) part of the Liturgy of the Hours'; it also specifically mentions that 'it is of great advantage for the family ... not only to pray together ... but also to celebrate some parts of the liturgy of the hours as occasion offers, in order to enter more deeply into the life of the Church' (*§27*).

Ideally, of course, it should be celebrated by a group of Christians together with their priest, and it is good to find such groups in various parts of the country: each group is the praying Church in that area. However, ideals cannot always be achieved and it would be tragic if an individual were to give up all idea of praying the Office because it was possible to find only one or two like-minded friends, or even impossible to find a single one. Father A-M Roguet OP, who helped to draft the General Instruction, points out that 'whether it be a group ... of lay people, or even a lay person on his (her) own – if they celebrate the Liturgy of the Hours, they are truly praying the prayer of the Church, with Christ, and their celebration is "liturgical" in the fullest sense of the word'[8]. Individual celebration, to quote the example given by Roguet, might be compared to the 'adaptation' of a symphony for a piano solo; though not as rich and rewarding an experience as it might be, nonetheless, it is a living out of the priestly character we acquired at baptism, by which we receive the vocation to sing the praises of God; it is genuine liturgical prayer and enjoys all the benefits that have been spoken of in this section.

The Whole Day for God

What's so special about this particular prayer? Fourthly, the fact that it sanctifies the day.

You will remember that the Second Vatican Council called for a renewal of the Office which would incorporate the soundest insights of contemporary scholarship. When the official edition of the new Office appeared in 1971, it carried as its first title – rather unexpectedly – 'The Liturgy of the Hours'. I suppose the term 'Office' is the one with which the majority of people are familiar, and it is still probably the one most commonly used, at least in the English-speaking world. And there is no reason why it should not continue to be used[9]. Nonetheless, it is worth noting that the title 'Liturgy of the Hours' has its own peculiar value in that it brings out a key feature of the Prayer of the Church: its potential for sanctifying the whole of our day and the whole of our life.

There is a lovely verse in Psalm 64 ('To you our praise is due') which runs as follows: 'The Lord crowns the year with his goodness.' So he does, but he also crowns every day, and every hour of every day, with his goodness. Through the Liturgy of the Hours the Church responds to that generous outpouring with a daily outpouring of its own, in prayers of praise, gratitude and petition addressed to God. Indeed 'by ancient Christian tradition what distinguishes the liturgy of the hours from other liturgical services is that it consecrates to God the whole cycle of the day and the night' (*GI§10*). In other words, it is a means of sanctifying the various hours that make up the day and all the activities that fill them; its different parts are intended to straddle the whole twenty-four hours rather than to be treated as a quota of prayers to be got through at all costs each day. It is recorded that Cardinal Richelieu was so busy, when he rose to high office of state in France, that it became his practice to spend from 11 pm to 1 am saying the Offices of two successive days, thus leaving himself almost two days completely free for other things![10] There is no sense in wrenching the Hours away from the various parts of the day to which they belong, bunching them together and then 'getting through' them in one spiritually indigestible lump.

After all, as we have explained, the purpose of the Liturgy of the Hours is to ensure that the whole course of the day may be overshadowed, as it were, and thereby hallowed and sanctified by the overarching prayer and praise of the Church. No precise times are laid down for the recitation of this or that particular Hour but 'so that the day may be truly sanctified and that the hours themselves may be recited with spiritual benefit, it is important that each canonical hour be recited as closely as possible to the time of day for which it is intended' (*CL §94*).

Like the early Church, the Church of today strives to respond to our Lord's precept 'about the need to pray continually and never lose heart' (*Luke 18:1*); it strives to heed the exhortation to 'offer God an unending sacrifice of praise' (*Hebrews 13:15*). The GI reminds us that 'the Church fulfils this precept (and responds to this exhortation) not only by celebrating the Eucharist, but in otherways also, especially through the liturgy of the hours' (*§10*). Of course most lay people, unless they are retired or sick or out of work, cannot be expected to follow the full cycle of the Office each day; but that does not mean that they might not be able to pray part of it, at least from time to time, either with other Christians or within their own family circle. Indeed, as we have seen, the Church gives them every encouragement to do so, and in particular to pray Morning and Evening Prayer (*see GI§ 27, and also §§ 21 to 23*).

Lessons in Prayer

What's so special about this particular prayer? Fifthly, the fact that it is a school of prayer.

This chapter has been concerned almost exclusively with public prayer, the Prayer of the Church. But it must not be imagined that public, liturgical prayer is unconnected with private, personal prayer; still less, that it is in competition with it and even threatens to replace it. On the contrary, the two belong together, the one enriching the other. And yet it must be admitted that at times they are not seen that way; so, for example, while it is usually assumed that a homily on prayer will be concerned exclusively with private prayer, it is similarly assumed that a talk on the liturgy will have little or nothing to do with how we pray!

It may be helpful therefore to consider each of the two types of prayer a little more closely. Strictly speaking, 'prayer is not in the first place something that we do in our various nooks and crannies, and then occasionally come together to do collectively; it is in the first place something that we do together, as the Church, so that even when we are alone it is still as members of the Church that we pray'[11]. Putting that another way: it is the Spirit, dwelling in the Church, who empowers the Church to pray, so that prayer is a joint enterprise of 'the Spirit and the Bride' (*Apocalypse 22:17*); and it is because the Church prays that we, as individuals, are able to pray. In the words of Eucharistic Prayer III, 'From age to age you gather a people to yourself, so that from the rising of the sun to its setting a pure offering may made to the glory of your name.' It has been suggested that love of the liturgy is an indication of spiritual growth, for the Holy Spirit tends to lead us into a prayer which is, as we have said, the prayer of Jesus to the Father; moreover, he tends to direct us to a deeper appreciation of that prayer, 'so we are led from an earlier stage of trying during the liturgy to concentrate on the meaning of words, that are out there ... to the point at which these are the words we really want to say, when the language of the liturgy is found within the heart'[12]. To some extent, the liturgy is a yardstick for private prayer, preventing it from becoming narrow, self-regarding, individualistic; it encourages us to be large-hearted, unselfish, concerned for others, to recognise that all Christian prayer has a trinitarian structure, that it encompasses praise and thanksgiving and penitence, as well as petition.

At the same time, we must not treat liturgical prayer as though it were self-sufficient: it almost inevitably lacks the spontaneity of private prayer; it may even lapse into a merely formal recitation of words and performance of actions. Private prayer helps to counteract such dangers and enable us to undertake liturgical prayer in a more sincere, more reflective frame of mine. Indeed, experience shows that, as a general rule, those who are committed to personal prayer are the ones who gain most from public liturgical prayer, and vice versa. There is clearly a complementarity between the two which should make us cautious about making too sharp a distinction between them. Paul VI expressly stated his hope that the new Office would 'pervade and renew the whole of Christian prayer, giving it life, direction and expression and effectively nourishing the spiritual life of the People of God' (*Laudis Canticum §8; emphasis added*). The devout public praying of the Office is 'a source of devotion' and a 'deepening of personal prayer' (*GI§19; emphasis added*); according to Crichton, 'one of the best features of the new office is that it has made possible a contemplative prayer of the hours'[13].

The daily use of even part of the Divine Office is a regular recalling of the bedrock truth which St Ignatius of Loyola called 'the first principle and foundation' of our spiritual lives, namely, that we have been created by God for no other purpose than that we may praise, reverence and serve him, and so attain the goal of eternal happiness with him in heaven. There is so much that distracts us from living out this truth, so many voices that tell us that we must get on with life and that prayer is a luxury we can ill afford, so many excuses that encourage us to reduce our prayer-life until it becomes little more than attendance at a Sunday service, and perhaps a mumbled prayer in the morning and evening. The Office teaches us that a characteristic trait of God's people has always been their readiness to turn to God in praise.

At the heart of the Office is the psalter, the book of psalms, which deserves the title of 'Universal Prayer Book', for in the course of human history no other has been used by so many men and women of so many different backgrounds, at so many different times and in so many different circumstances. It has even (one is tempted to say 'especially') been used by people in terrible suffering or danger, such as the victims of the concentration camps in Germany and Russia. In her splendid account of her time in captivity, the Russian dissident poet Irina Ratushinskaya describes what happened when she and her two friends were placed in 'shizo' (the harsh regime of a punishment cell): 'Galya and Pani Lida had already become a very accomplished duet at singing psalms and hymns, and what better occupation can there be in a SHIZO cell than to praise the Lord? The regime supervisors ... stormed and threatened, but ... Pani Lida and Galya were both perfectly prepared to accept punishment for singing psalms'[14].

However, the psalter's universality refers not only to the countless hosts of people who have had recourse to it throughout the ages, but also to the breadth and richness of its contents: every human emotion seems to have its place there. To take some examples almost at random, there is the heartfelt longing of: 'Like the deer that yearns for running streams, so my soul is yearning for you, my God'; the bitter anguish of: 'My God, my God, why have you forsaken me?'; the craving for forgiveness of: 'Have mercy on me, God, in your kindness, in your compassion blot out my offence'; the unalloyed bliss of: 'What marvels the Lord worked for us! Indeed we were glad'; the sheer desolation of: 'My one companion is darkness'; the yearning for God to be universally praised of: 'Let everything that lives and breathes give praise to the Lord'; the utter trust of: 'Your love reaches to the heavens, your truth (steadfastness) to the skies'; the joyous gratitude of: 'It is good to give thanks to the Lord, to make music to your name, O Most High'[15]. All the great themes of prayer weave their way through the verses of the psalms, and underlying them all there is an extraordinary awareness of the reality of God and of the need to turn to him in prayer. Of course, there are lots of grumbles – and worse! – as we shall see, for the psalmists were not afraid to speak their minds – and hearts. Nonetheless, there is no mistaking the profound clinging to God that is evident everywhere in the book of psalms. It is difficult to see how we can pray these psalms day by day without being profoundly influenced by them, without becoming more deeply prayerful people.

However, the Office consists not only of psalms but also of many other Scriptural readings, excerpts taken from various parts of the Old and New Testaments. That is important, for it underlines the fact that all prayer presupposes a knowledge of God: I must know something of him, which in turn means that he must have revealed himself, before I am in a position to turn to him in prayer. He has in fact revealed himself, he has spoken to us, especially in the Scriptures and supremely in Jesus, but we need to hear him speaking again in our own day; in the words of the psalm: 'O that today you would listen to his voice' (*94:7*). In the readings of the liturgy, including the psalms themselves, that need is met, for it is there that God 'speaks' to us once again. This is how CL puts it: 'in the liturgy God speaks to his people, Christ is still proclaiming his Gospel' (*§33*). This divine initiative obviously calls for a response on our part, and so the Constitution continues: 'And the people respond to God both in song and prayer'. Thus, 'in a celebration in common and in private recitation, the essential structure of this liturgy remains the same, that is, it is a conversation between God and his people' (*GI§33*). In other words, it is a dialogue between God and us.

Drawing together the threads of this chapter, we can see why the Prayer of the Church is of such importance: it is a prayer which reflects the community nature of the Church; a Trinitarian prayer enabling us, through the power of the Spirit, to participate in Christ's own worship of the Father; a liturgical prayer which extends the effects of the Eucharist throughout the day, continuing the saving work of Christ and empowering us to bring down God's blessing on all humankind; a prayer whose purpose it is to sanctify the hours of day and night with all their activities. The more we reflect on the nature of the Office, the better we shall appreciate that it is not only prayer but a school of prayer, or as Robert Taft has described it, 'a novitiate in which (the Church) teaches her age-old ways of how to glorify God in Christ as Church'[16]. And it will surely come as no surprise to discover that the opening words of the General Instruction on the Liturgy of the Hours run as follows: 'Public and common prayer by the people of God is rightly considered to be among the primary duties of the Church' (*§1*).

But now the time has come to enquire: how then, in practical terms, are we to go about the praying of the Prayer of the Church? It is to that topic that we turn in chapter three.

References

1. From the title of chapter 22 of *The Liturgy of the Hours in East and West* Liturgical Press, Collegeville, Minnesota, (1986)

2. D Adams *The Eye of the Eagle* SPCK, London (1990) p45

3. S Tugwell OP *Prayer* Veritas Publications, Dublin (1976) p65

4. Y Congar OP *The Mystery of the Church* London & Baltimore, (1960) p70

5. 'Praying the Divine Office' in *Liturgy* (1980) – p7

6. In Pius XII's ground-breaking encyclical on the Liturgy, *Mediator Dei* (1947)

7. *Catechism of the Catholic Church* (1994) Geoffrey Chapman – §1178

8. His book, *The Liturgy of the Hours: the General Instruction with Commentary* was published in 1971 by the Liturgical Press, Collegeville, Minnesota. It has inspired a good deal of this section.

9. In fact the expression 'Office' (or 'Divine Office'), though not mentioned in the first place, is also used.

10. A Martimort *The Church at Prayer* Liturgical Press, Collegeville, Minnesota (1985) p177

11. S Tugwell OP *op.cit.* pp.60-61

12. P Hocken *You He Made Alive* Darton, Longman & Todd, London (1974) p45

13. J D Crichton *Understanding the Prayer of the Church* Geoffrey Chapman (1992) p12 (emphasis added)

14. *Grey is the Colour of Hope* Hodder & Stoughton, p327

15. The references are psalms 41:2; 21:2; 50:3; 125:3; 87:19; 150:6; 56:11 and 91:1.

16. R Taft *The Liturgy of the Hours in East and West* p368

3 – Praying the Prayer of the Church (i) – Morning and Evening Prayer

'Day begins to the music of a psalm. Day closes to the echo of a psalm.' (St Ambrose +397)

'One can live for some days without eating, but not without praying. Prayer is the key of the morning and the bolt of the evening.' (Mahatma Gandhi +1948)

It may seem like a statement of the obvious to observe that the Prayer of the Church is above all else prayer. But if so, it is also a statement of the most important truth of all, for unless we give priority to the prayer value of the Office, we shall run the risk of a spiritual anorexia: we may feed faithfully on the celebration of the Office day by day but it will fail to nourish our relationship with the Lord, and with our brothers and sisters, in the way it should. It is the Prayer of the Church; our task is to appropriate it and make it our prayer also. It is not simply a portion of words to be got through, but rather, if one may put it this way, a partner intended to be spiritually profitable to ourselves, to the Church at large and indeed to the whole human race.

One indication of the GI's concern for the prayerful nature of the Office is that it devotes a whole section to 'Sacred Silence'. Following the general principle laid down by CL§30, it points out that within the celebration of the Prayer of the Church there should be times for observing 'a reverent silence' (*§201*) – not a bleak emptiness with nothing happening, but a time of expectation, of waiting upon God. It is sad when a liturgical service is all noise and chatter, when it is treated like a rocket on its launch-pad in that once lift-off from the launchpad is achieved, the operation must continue uninterrupted on its course. We have already seen that liturgical worship is a dialogue, a two-way process, between God and ourselves. Viewed in that light, silence is not an interruption but an integral part of the rhythm of that process: public worship demands times for speaking and singing, but also times for being silent, for listening, for deepening our appreciation of what is said or sung, for allowing ourselves to be touched by the Lord. Indeed, CL§30 implies that silence is for developing 'active participation' in the liturgy. Of course it would be disastrous in public celebration of the Office – or of the Mass, for that matter – to go to the other extreme, by introducing silences indiscriminately or prolonging them unduly. But, provided the congregation knows in advance, a brief silence after, say, a psalm or a scriptural reading – two points where silence is expressly suggested by the GI (*see §202*) – would serve to enhance the prayerful atmosphere of the Office.

Prayer that is a Partnership

We spoke of the Prayer of the Church in terms of partnership, but partnerships have to be worked at. They require commitment, a commitment that can perhaps be spelled out in terms of fidelity, the giving of time and at least a minimum of appreciation, affection, love. It seems to me that those three factors – fidelity, time and love – play a part in any spiritually successful partnership with the Prayer of the Church, though in practice they tend to merge one with another – and, as we shall see, the love element will often arrive last of all and come as a result of the other two.

I speak of fidelity because the Prayer of the Church is in large measure an acquired taste. Of course a one-off involvement in, say, Morning Prayer can whet a person's appetite for the Office, and it is significant that the 'Order of Christian Funerals' offers Morning or Evening Prayer as an optional element of funeral liturgies. However, as a rule, the Office will yield its full riches to those who are faithful to it day after day, in good times as well as bad, rather than to those who turn to it occasionally or only when they are in the mood. For those who are deputed to pray the whole Office there is an additional need for fidelity, though in a somewhat different sense. The distinguishing feature of the

Liturgy of the Hours (see above p38ff) is that, by being spread across the day, it consecrates the twenty-four hours to God. And so fidelity to the nature of the prayer implies that its various Hours are 'staggered' so that they do in fact straddle the day from dawn to dusk and, by the same token, that priority is given to the 'two hinges' of the Office, namely, Morning and Evening Prayer.

What has been said about daily fidelity to the Prayer of the Church leads on to the second contribution to our partnership with the Prayer of the Church – the giving of time, that most precious of all our possessions. Few things are so inimical to prayer of any kind, not least to the Office – this applies especially to those who pray it on their own – as that of trying to fit it in during odd moments or trying to get through it as quickly as possible. When St Teresa of Avila was asked by one of her sisters how she ought to pray, the saint replied: 'Sister, pray the Our Father – but take an hour to say it.' If we are going to pray, and not simply say, the Prayer of the Church, then as with all prayer, we need to try and find a conducive atmosphere, a place which is favourable to prayer; we need to be recollected, free as far as possible from the distracting thoughts that crowd into our minds; and we need time, for the Office is too good to rush. (An interesting little experiment might be to see how long it will be before you slip into the habit – or resist the temptation – of arranging the ribbons of the breviary or zipping it up or fastening its buttons while still in the process of saying 'through Jesus Christ etc'! It's just one of the many small ways which can betray undue haste.)

The more we are faithful to the Prayer of the Church, day by day and down through the years, the more we are willing to devote adequate time to it, the more we shall become attached to it; life would somehow be empty without it. In simple, straightforward language, the Office becomes 'The Prayer we have learned to love' and, like anything (or anyone) else we love, it begins to colour our lives, to influence our thoughts and outlook, often in subtle ways, to become in a sense part of ourselves. This is why the GI, in the spirit of CL§26, promises that a 'worthy, attentive, and devout' celebration of the Liturgy of the Hours, where 'mind and voice (are) in harmony', becomes 'a source of devotion, a means of gaining God's manifold grace, a deepening of personal prayer, and an incentive to the work of the apostolate' (*§19*).

Finally, here are a few simple strategems that have been found helpful in the praying of the Office, especially by those who do so on their own. But remember that they are only aids, or possible aids, to prayer: nothing can replace the hard slog that all praying sometimes demands. Moreover, I recognise that for some people it is difficult, if not impossible – because of their circumstances or because of prior responsibilities – to devote to the Prayer of the Church as much time and attention as they would wish; I am equally convinced that the Lord will more than make up to you for your efforts, providing you do your best. Other people, however, are not so constrained and it is they who may most benefit from some of the following ten suggestions:

i) Make up your mind where you are going to pray and prepare the place before you begin. So, for example, if the venue is to be your room, try and make it as conducive to prayer as possible. If there's a 'phone there, then that certainly has to go off! A strategically placed crucifix or icon or lighted candle can help to create the right atmosphere. Make sure that the markers in your book are set in advance and won't have to be sought for during prayer time; similarly, where various options are offered (e.g. re hymns), make your choice before the prayer begins; be clear in your own mind what you are going to use, e.g. a bible or a hymnal, and ensure that it is to hand.

ii) Whenever we are about to embark upon an action of some moment, it is natural that we steady ourselves for what lies ahead. And so do not rush into the praying of the Office; give yourself a couple of moments to reflect on what you are about to do, to collect your thoughts, to settle your heart. An initial sign of the cross made with some deliberation can prove an excellent first step. Another helpful practice is to stand up for the introduction 'O God, come to our aid…' and the 'Glory be to the Father' in order to make the point to yourself that now you are entering a time of prayer.

iii) If the verse of a psalm or a sentence in a scriptural reading strikes you, dwell on it for a brief while; it may be a thought that you can carry with you and that you will be happy to return to from time to time throughout the day.

iv) Occasionally you might be able to treat yourself by devoting perhaps ten minutes or more to a psalm so that it begins to seep into your bones. This seems to have been in the mind of Cardinal Hume, when as Abbot of Ampleforth he urged his monks 'to spend quite a lot of time looking at, mulling over, really questioning the psalms'[1]. There are some psalms that look as though they may never fire you, but, surprisingly, a psalm that has meant very little in the past can suddenly burst open with meaning. When that happens its effects are felt in your approach to all the other psalms. 'One of the best ways to learn to appreciate the Psalms is to acquire the habit of reciting them slowly and well'[2].

v) Using another translation of the psalms may bring a freshness to your prayer; it may also lead to the discovery of helpful images or expressions which did not appear in the familiar version. For similar reasons, if you have a foreign language, why not sometimes use that in the Office? It too may reveal some aspect of the psalms which you were unaware of.

vi) GI*§110* notes that one of the elements that has 'greatly contributed to an understanding of the psalms and their use as Christian prayer' has been 'psalm-prayers'. As far back as the fourth century it was customary to pause after the praying of a psalm to give time for reflection and also to prevent undue haste. The time of silence was broken by a 'psalm-prayer' – an improvised collect-type prayer spoken by the one presiding. A collection of such prayers has been gathered by Brian Magee in his book *Psalm Prayers for Morning and Evening Prayer.* The use of such prayers can be a valuable way of enriching our approach to the psalms and canticles.

vii) A suitable holy picture, say Rembrandt's 'Prodigal Son', slipped into the pages of the breviary – and replaced from time to time – may serve as a focus for your thoughts and prayers. A 'seasonal image', one that will remind you of the current season of the Church's year – Advent, Christmas, Lent, Easter – can be particularly supportive as you pray the Prayer of the Church.

viii) If you learn a few psalms – your favourite ones – by heart, not only can you then use them whenever you wish, but they will meet you like welcome old friends when they turn up in the Office.

ix) It isn't only complete psalms that can with profit be learned by heart but also excerpts from them. The fact is that the psalter is like a quiver holding an endless supply of arrow-like prayers that can be sent up to God at any time of day or night, such as: 'How great is your name, Lord God, through all the earth' (*8:2*), or 'Lord, make me know your ways. Lord, teach me your paths' (*24:4*), or 'The Lord is my strength and my song; he is my saviour' (*117,14*).

x) Another way of drawing your attention to what the Office has to offer is to underline, with a soft pencil, a phrase, or even a word, that attracts you, or a couple of lines in a psalm which are repeated chorus-like.

Prayer that is Flexible

Another aid to the praying of the Prayer of the Church is the recognition that one of the goals of Vatican II was to promote a living liturgy, a liturgy which is supple and diverse, a liturgy which allows for, even encourages, a certain amount of freedom in its celebration. And so the fidelity we spoke of earlier must not be confused with inflexibility. Indeed the GI insists that the celebration must not be 'too inflexible... nor concerned merely with the formal observance of rules... (and that its) primary aim must be to inspire hearts with a desire for genuine prayer and to show that the celebration of God's praise is a thing of joy' (*§279*)[3]. Obviously, there is greater freedom of choice on an ordinary weekday than there is on a day which has its own specially arranged texts, such as a Sunday or a solemn feastday or one of the major seasons of the Church's liturgical year; similarly there is much greater freedom of choice for those who pray on their own or with one or two others than for those who take part in an official service. However, the important fact is that, within the basic framework and spirit of the various Hours, there is considerable room for adaptation and choice. Thus, a longer reading or a more suitable one, such as that of the day's Mass, may replace the short reading in the breviary; again, where a long psalm is divided up (for example, at Evening Prayer), the whole psalm may be read straight through. These are just a couple of examples; many more will become apparent as you become familiar with the Prayer of the Church.

Where the Office is being prayed by an individual or by, say, a small group, it will be even easier to introduce flexibility. For instance, there might be longer silences after the psalms; individuals might be invited to repeat (without comment) a word or phrase in the psalm or in the reading that seemed to speak powerfully to them; there might be a homily after the Reading and the homily might be shared, so that everyone present would be free, if they so desired, to make a personal contribution.

Again, the celebration of the Office could take place within a period of Exposition of the Blessed Sacrament or during Holy Hour. The GI (*§93-98*) explains how Morning or Evening Prayer may also be incorporated into the Mass; it is arranged as follows:

i) the two psalms and canticle;

ii) the Gloria (where appropriate), followed by the opening prayer of the Mass;

iii) the Readings of the Mass, followed by the Intercessions from the Office (or, on Sunday, by the Prayer of the Faithful);

iv) the Mass continues as usual until after Communion, when the Benedictus or (in the evening) the Magnificat is said or sung;

v) final prayer of the Mass and usual ending.

Recent documents have suggested the use of Morning and Evening Prayer not only as part of the 'Order of Christian Funerals' (see page 46) but also for Sunday or weekday celebration in places where there is no priest to celebrate Mass: the 'possibility should always be kept in mind of celebrating a part of the Liturgy of the Hours, e.g. Morning or Evening Prayer, in which the appropriate Sunday readings may be included... At the end of such a celebration, Communion may be celebrated'[4].

Prayer that is Celebration

Liturgy is more than words: it is action, it is celebration, it is the worship of a community. It is because the Prayer of the Church is liturgy, and not simply a private devotional exercise, that it ought to be, as far as possible, a celebration. Thus, the whole celebrating group makes the sign of the cross at the beginning of the Hour and again at the gospel canticles, the *Benedictus* (at Morning Prayer) and *Magnificat* (at Evening Prayer); they stand for the gospel canticles, as well as for the hymn and the short responsory; as at Mass, different people should play different roles: leading the celebration, proclaiming the Scripture reading and so on. In particular, singing should be encouraged; singing not only of the hymn but also of the psalms and canticles – after all, they were originally composed as songs and, now incorporated into the Prayer of the Church, they are still meant to be sung. The GI makes it clear that singing is more than a mere embellishment superimposed upon the Office: it is the natural way of expressing our praise and joy. It is also the best way of revealing the communal nature of Christian prayer, and so 'all the people of God' should be encouraged 'to join together in singing the hours in a spirit of joy, especially on Sundays and holy days'(*§270*).

At the same time, the GI is realistic enough to recognise the need for what it calls a 'progressive solemnity'. In simple terms, that means two things. First, the more solemn the occasion the more appropriate it is that there should be singing (as well as other distinctive features, such as will be mentioned in the next paragraph). It produces a 'flattening' of the Prayer of the Church to present it always in the same fashion, so that there is no obvious difference between the celebration of the greatest feast and that of an ordinary day of the year. Thus, singing is more appropriate at the Sunday Office than at a weekday's; or on a festival day than on an ordinary day; or at the pivotal Hours of Morning and Evening Prayer than at other Hours. Secondly, account has to be taken of 'the number of singers available in the circumstances' – and how well they can sing! Better a prayerfully recited Office than a badly sung one. Initially, at any rate, the aim might be to have just the hymn and Gospel canticle sung, and then, when people have become more confident, to introduce the singing of at least some of the psalms, especially those of praise.

There are other ways in which a celebratory atmosphere can be created at Morning and Evening Prayer, especially on Sundays and important festivals. For example, the celebrant might wear a cope; there might be a procession, with lighted candles, through the church at the beginning and end of the celebration; a thurible and incense might be used. One of the most attractive features of Evening Prayer in days gone by must have been the Service of Light with which the Hour began. Originally a practical measure – it was already getting dark, people needed a light to see by – it came to be looked upon as a symbol of Christ the Light of the World; from possibly as early as the second century, it was accompanied by a beautiful hymn, 'O gladdening light'. Another ritual commonly used was the burning of incense, whose ascending smoke symbolised prayer and was associated with Psalm 140 ('I have called to you, Lord, hasten to help me'), a psalm which begs: 'O Lord, let my prayer rise before you like incense.'

A similar rite has been reintroduced in some churches today, and there is much to be said for it. It would be suitable for special occasions; and the Paschal candle or one of the Advent candles (or one of those branched Benediction candle-holders, resurrected from a sacristy cupboard) could be solemnly lit, accompanied by a suitable hymn. The rest of the Office could follow, though it would be good to replace one of the psalms with Psalm 140, accompanied by an incensing of the whole congregation. It might even be wise on this special occasion to reduce the two psalms and canticle to just Psalm 140 on its own so that the service would not be unduly prolonged.

This is an example of what can be done. No doubt, in the years ahead there will be further experimentation, leading to the discovery of other ways of making Morning and Evening Prayer a real celebration. But the ultimate hope must surely be that the Prayer of the Church at the beginning and end of the day will become a popular prayer service of the People of God, so that once again it will come to be known as the 'People's Office'.

The 'Mechanics' of the Office

I have spoken of flexibility in the celebration of the Office. However, that must not blind us to the fact that the Prayer of the Church is a given. Like all liturgy, it is not something that we put together for ourselves, in accordance with our own quirks or moods, but essentially something that we receive from God through his Church. Flexibility, therefore, takes place within a definite framework, and anyone who wishes to pray the Office must be familiar with that framework, must understand what I call the 'mechanics' of the Office.

Explaining those mechanics by means of the written word may seem like trying to explain in print how to drive a car. It can make a relatively simple operation sound needlessly complex: strange words – like responsories and antiphons, canticles and liturgical seasons, versicles and responses – crop up; a confusing variety of alternatives is sometimes offered; and the at-first-sight daunting art of shuttling to and fro through the pages of the Office book has to be mastered. In fact, far better than learning the mechanics via the written word is having someone on the spot who is familiar with the breviary, especially if he or she is willing to pray the Office with you in the early days and later to serve as a resource to whom you can turn, should you meet with difficulties. However, not everyone has such a friend and, besides, the good news is that, like driving a car, praying the Divine Office quickly becomes second nature, so that after a short time you should have got well beyond the L-plate stage. Furthermore, there is no need to attempt everything at once: if you are approaching the Prayer of the Church for the first time, you might find it helpful, for example, to begin by using just one psalm instead of three in Morning Prayer and Evening Prayer, and then go on to the Our Father and the final prayer. Once you feel at ease with that you can make progress to the other parts of the Hour.

Morning and Evening Prayer

In this chapter we are confining ourselves to the mechanics of just two Hours of the Office, Morning and Evening Prayer, the two Hours which are, as we saw in the last chapter, 'the two hinges on which the (whole) daily Office turns' (*CL§89*). The GI comments that they are 'to be accorded the highest importance as the prayer of the Christian community. Their public or communal celebration should be encouraged ... Indeed, the recitation of these prayers should be recommended also to individual members of the faithful unable to participate in a celebration in common' (*§40*).

Just as we restrict our concern in this chapter to the two principal parts of the Prayer of the Church, so too, in the interests of simplicity, we shall deal only with their major features, leaving more detailed considerations for the Postscript at the end. The basic pattern of both Hours is the same, as this diagram shows:

Morning Prayer		**Evening Prayer**
	INTRODUCTION & HYMN	
	PSALMS	
Morning Psalm		First Psalm
Old Testament Canticle		Second Psalm
Second Psalm		New Testament Canticle
	SCRIPTURE READING	
Gospel Canticle (of Zechariah)		Gospel Canticle (of Mary)
	INTERCESSIONS	
Consecrating day to God		Petitions for the needs of world
	LORD'S PRAYER	
	FINAL PRAYER AND BLESSING	

The Introduction takes the form of an appeal to God for help – he is even urged to hurry! – 'O God, come to our aid; Lord, make haste to help us.' It is accompanied by the sign of the cross, the sign which is an acknowledgement of the redeeming work of our Lord's death and resurrection, by which we become sharers in the life of Father, Son and Holy Spirit; and is followed by the 'doxology' (= song of praise): 'Glory be to the Father, etc'. And so from the outset it is made clear that prayer is more than a man (or woman)-sized affair: it is in fact impossible without God's help. 'Without me,' said Jesus, 'you can do nothing' (*John 15:5*), and this is peculiarly so in the case of prayer, for all Christian prayer is a sharing in the prayer of Christ.

The opening sign of the cross and doxology are followed by a Hymn which, like the entrance hymn at Mass, invites us to worship and at the same time puts us into an appropriate frame of mind. It expresses the 'flavour' of the particular Hour or feast and helps to draw us into its celebration (*GI§42 and 174*). A fine example is the hymn suggested for Morning Prayer of Sunday in Weeks One and Three, 'Transcendent God in whom we live', with its reference to the end of the night, the morning cock-crow and morning hymn, the resurrection, as well as praise of God who called us out of nothingness and in whom alone we can find our resting place. 'With gratitude in your hearts,' says one of the earliest Christian writings, 'sing psalms and hymns and inspired songs' (*Colossians 3:16*); and St Augustine used to claim that 'to sing is to pray twice'! The kind of singing referred to is that of a congregation and so, in celebrating on one's own, the hymn may be omitted. Nonetheless, I know one or two people who are quite happy to sing a hymn on their own – even if they judge it wise to do so *sotto voce*.

A generous assortment of hymns is available in the breviary and some are deeply inspiring. Sheila Cassidy has written[5]: 'I am constantly amazed at the richness of the Divine Office. I love the hymns especially for their poetry and their pure theology'; and she adds: 'The psalms and hymns seem to work as a sort of magic carpet carrying me to God when my wordless imageless chariot fails' (*emphasis added*). Favourite hymns, like favourite poems, are largely a matter of personal taste, but one of my 'magic carpets' is the hymn that the breviary offers us for Morning Prayer on Friday of Week Three, a great Trinitarian hymn which casts the spotlight, in turn, upon Father, Son and Holy

Spirit and on what each has done in the work of our salvation, and ends with a paean of praise:

We bless you, Father, Lord of Life,
To whom all living beings tend,
The source of holiness and grace,
Our first beginning and our end.

We give you thanks, Redeeming Christ,
Who bore our weight of sin and shame;
In dark defeat you conquered sin
And death, by dying, overcame.

Come, Holy Spirit, searching fire,
Whose flame all evil burns away.
Come down to us with light and love,
In silence and in peace to stay.

We praise you, Trinity in One,
Sublime in majesty and might,
Who reign for ever, Lord of all,
In splendour and unending light.

The Psalms stand at the heart of the Divine Office. They are arranged in such a way that in the course of a four-week cycle (see Appendix II), all one hundred and fifty of them, except for a tiny handful which are omitted because of their 'imprecatory (cursing) character' (*GI§131*), appear in one or other of the Hours. The monthly psalm-cycle is coordinated with the liturgical year so that (even though one or more Weeks of a given cycle may be omitted) it always begins again at Week I on:

the First Sunday of Advent
the First Sunday in Ordinary Time
the First Sunday of Lent
and on Easter Sunday.

The next chapter deals expressly with the psalms, but at this point we need to be aware of the part they play in Morning Prayer and Evening Prayer, for in each of these Hours there are two psalms, as well as a psalm-like poem or canticle. The latter comes from a biblical book other than the psalter, but for all practical purposes can be treated as another psalm. The morning canticle is taken from the Old Testament, the evening one from the New. The former is sandwiched between the two psalms, because like them it comes from the Old Testament; but the latter, because it comes from the New, appropriately follows the psalms. (The use of Old Testament canticles at Morning Prayer has a long history in the Church, but the use of those from the New Testament is a happy innovation of Vatican II.)

Morning Prayer is meant to sanctify the new day. St Basil the Great, who was a monk, a hermit and then bishop of Caesarea (a few miles north of present day Haifa) until his death in 379, expressed it in these words: Morning Prayer 'is said ... in order that the first stirrings of our mind and will may be consecrated to God and that we may take nothing in hand until we have been gladdened by the thought of God ...' (*quoted in GI§38*). (Admittedly, Basil seems to have had his brother-monks in mind; many people may manage a brief prayer when they arise, but are unable to tackle anything more, such as Morning Prayer, until later. But even then it retains the purpose Basil spoke of.) The first psalm of Morning Prayer often reflects the notion of a new day. For example, Psalm 5 ('To my words give ear, O Lord'), prayed on Monday Morning of Week One, catches the mood in the words: 'In the <u>morning</u> you hear me; in the <u>morning</u> I offer you my prayer'; similarly, Psalm 142 ('Lord, listen to my prayer'), used on Thursday morning of Week Four, looks forward in hope to the new day: 'In the <u>morning</u> let me know your love for I put my trust in you. Make me know the way I should walk' (in the course of this coming day). Again, Psalm 56 ('Have mercy on me, God, have mercy'), used on Thursday morning of Week One, clearly has the new day in mind; the psalmist imagines himself, as only a poet can, first of all waking up, then waking up lyre and harp so that they and he together may finally awaken the dawn! 'My heart is ready, O God, my heart is ready. I will sing ... your praise. <u>Awake</u> my soul, <u>awake</u> lyre and harp, I will <u>awake</u> the dawn' (all emphases in this paragraph have been added).

Traditionally, Morning Prayer has also been linked with the resurrection: at the time of the rising of the sun, our thoughts turn to Jesus, the Light of the World, who has risen on high from his tomb to enlighten every human creature on the face of the earth. St Cyprian, who died in 258, states concisely: 'There should be prayer in the morning so that the resurrection of the Lord may thus be celebrated' (*quoted in GI§38*). Not surprisingly, then, the second psalm of Morning Prayer is usually one of praise, the most appropriate prayer to offer him who has risen from the dead and who is to be greeted as Lord. In fact praise has been so closely associated with this Hour of the Divine Office that, as was indicated in chapter 2, throughout the history of the Church the name by which it has most commonly been known is that of 'Lauds', which is simply the Latin for 'praises'. Psalm 150, ('Praise God in his holy place'), which is the second psalm for Morning Prayer of Sunday of Week One, is a fine example of a psalm of praise, but many more are to be found in the Liturgy of the Hours.

The dominant theme of Evening Prayer is thanksgiving for the blessings of the day that has gone; but just as Morning Prayer has a second theme, that of the resurrection of our Lord, so Evening Prayer with the accompanying darkness has a second theme, that of his passion; and the double theme is sometimes taken up by the psalms of the Hour. A striking example is found in Psalm 140 ('I have called to you, Lord; hasten to help me') which is the first psalm for Evening Prayer I of Sunday of Week One. (For Jews the Sabbath begins before sunset on the eve of the Sabbath; in similar fashion, according to ancient Christian tradition, Sunday, the Lord's Day, begins on Saturday evening. Hence, Sunday has two Evening Prayers – Evening Prayer I on Saturday and Evening Prayer II on Sunday.) Psalm 140 includes the words: 'Let my prayer come before you like incense, the raising of my hands like an evening oblation', and so contains a reference both to prayer in the evening and also to sacrifice. However, the prayer and the evening sacrifice which took place in the Temple at Jerusalem – and that is what the psalmist is referring to – are but a shadow of the Prayer and Great Sacrifice which took place in the paschal mystery on Good Friday afternoon.

<u>A Scripture Reading</u>, usually taken from the Old Testament at Morning Prayer and from the New Testament at Evening Prayer, follows the psalms. Despite its brevity – in fact a longer reading, such as that of the Mass of the day, may be used (*GI§46*) – 'it is to be read and received as a true

proclamation of the word of God' (*GI§45*). It may throw into relief an arresting scriptural phrase or an idea which would scarcely be noticed if it figured as part of a longer reading. Different Scripture Readings are provided not only for the different seasons and feasts of the Church's year, but for each of the days of the four weeks that make up the monthly liturgical cycle. And so a rich variety of scriptural reading is available to those who pray the breviary day by day. This is very much in accord with the emphasis which the Second Vatican Council placed on the importance of the Word of God for preaching and for liturgy, and also for the spiritual life of the People of God. Moreover, when the Prayer of the Church is celebrated with a congregation a brief homily may follow the reading to amplify its meaning.

After the reading a Short Responsory may be used; its purpose is to help us to turn the Reading just heard into personal prayer. In its printed form, it looks like this:

Short Responsory
℟ My helper is my God; I will place my trust in him. Repeat ℟
℣ He is my refuge; he sets me free. ℟ Glory be. ℟

It consists of three elements: first, a response ('My helper is my God; I will place my trust in him'), second, a versicle, or brief verse ('He is my refuge; he sets me free') and, third, the first part of the 'Glory be to the Father'. Thus, initially the response is repeated; then, after the versicle, it is repeated again; and finally, after the 'Glory be to the Father', it is repeated once more. Clearly, it is meant to be sung – if not sung, it may be omitted – with the 'Cantor', or lead singer, beginning, and then 'All' (i.e. the congregation), responding.

Gospel Canticle The chief distinguishing feature of a canticle is, as we have seen, that it does not belong to the book of psalms; instead, it comes from one of the other biblical books. Moreover, whereas the precise context of a psalm is almost invariably unknown (we do not know who composed it, or in what circumstances it was composed), the context of a canticle – and here we come to the second distinguishing feature of a canticle – is revealed in the book to which it belongs. This is clearly the case for the Gospel Canticles which are said, or sung, at Morning Prayer and Evening Prayer. They are called Gospel canticles because they come from the Gospels, rather than from any other New Testament writing. We need only turn to the first chapter of Luke to discover that the Morning Gospel Canticle (*1:68-79*) is the prayer of Zechariah, the husband of Elizabeth, and that it was uttered when their son, John the Baptist, was brought to the Temple to be circumcised and named. Similarly, that same chapter of Luke confirms that the Evening Gospel Canticle (*1:46-55*) is the joyous song of praise of our Lady on the occasion of her Visitation to Elizabeth.

These two Canticles are especially appropriate for the beginning and end of the day; the first because it speaks of 'the loving-kindness of the heart of our God who visits us like the dawn from on high', and reminds us that during this day we, like the Baptist, are each called to be 'a prophet of the Most High' and 'prepare his ways before him'; the second because its spirit of joy, gratitude and praise is the spirit in which we ought to end our day. The Benedictus and the Magnificat, to give them the names by which they are commonly known (each name comes from the opening word of the Latin version of the respective canticle), mark the high-point of the two Hours. Because their 'home', their place of origin, is in the Gospel, they are treated, at least in formal celebrations, with the same respect as is accorded to the proclamation of the Gospel at Mass: they are sung standing and their opening words are accompanied by the sign of the cross.

<u>Intercessions:</u> 'The celebration of the liturgy of the hours is praise of God. Yet Jewish and Christian tradition does not separate prayer of petition from praise of God' (*GI§179*): the one tends to lead to the other. St Paul is clear that we ought to offer 'supplications, intercessions and thanksgivings ... for everyone' (*1 Timothy 2:1*). And so in both Morning and Evening Prayer there is a series of intercessions. Like the Prayer of the Faithful at Mass, they broaden our vision by moving the centre of interest from ourselves and our needs to those of the whole human race. In addition to prayers for others, the morning intercessions are usually designed to dedicate the day that is just beginning by placing it in God's

hands, while the evening ones lay stress on thanksgiving, though the final one is always a prayer for the dead.
In the Office book, the printed intercessions look like this:

Intercessions
As Christians called to share the life of God, let us praise the Lord Jesus, the high priest of our faith. ℟ You are our Saviour and our God.
Almighty King, you have baptised us, and made us a royal priesthood: – may we offer you a constant sacrifice of praise. ℟
Help us to keep your commandments; – so that through your Holy Spirit we may dwell in you, and you in us. ℟
Everlasting Wisdom, come to us: – dwell with us and work in us today. ℟
Help us to be considerate and kind; – grant that we may bring joy, not pain, to those we meet. ℟

They can be recited in different ways. In private recitation all will obviously be said by the individual, though there is no reason why it cannot be shortened, for example, by reducing the repetitions. In public recitation, the one who presides may say all of the petitions and the congregation respond each time with the brief response which appears at the end of the first petition ('You are our Saviour and our God'); or, after the first intercession, the one presiding may say only the first part of the subsequent petitions (up to the hyphen), leaving the congregation to say the second part – with or without the initial response. Another possibility is for a reader to introduce all the intercessions apart from the first one, and he/she can do this in either of the ways just mentioned. It is possible to add further intentions of one's own (*GI§181*) or to observe a period of silence.

The Lord's Prayer According to St Augustine, 'Whatever other words we may say ... if we are praying in the right way, we say nothing that has not already a place in the Lord's prayer.' You may remember that one of our earliest records (see page 13) makes it clear that Christians used to recite the Lord's prayer three times each day; it is fascinating to see how that practice is maintained in the Church, for 'the Lord's Prayer will be said with solemnity on three occasions during the day: at Mass, at morning prayer and at evening prayer' (*GI§146*).

Conclusion The Hour is completed by a concluding prayer, followed immediately by a blessing. If a priest or deacon presides, there is the usual greeting and response: 'The Lord be with you', 'And also with you', followed by the blessing and the customary words of dismissal. If neither priest nor deacon is present, the blessing is imparted with these words: 'The Lord bless us and keep us from all evil, and bring us to everlasting life. Amen.'

Which Book to Use?

Before concluding this chapter, a word or two about the book you use in praying the Prayer of the Church. In fact several different kinds are available. First, there is the 'Divine Office', which is a translation of the full latin text; its size – it runs to three fairly hefty volumes – is almost entirely due to the fact that it includes the Office of Readings, incorporating lengthy excerpts both from Scripture and from Christian writers, for every single day of the year. Second comes 'Daily Prayer' which is almost identical with the complete breviary just described, but, because it omits the Office of Readings, consists of a single volume. Finally, there are two books which are specifically designed for those, especially the laity, who would find the complete breviary too demanding in terms of time required (though they are also valued by people who normally do pray the entire Office but, from time to time, need a shorter pocket version, for example, as a travelling companion). These two office books are entitled, respectively, 'Morning and Evening Prayer' and 'A Shorter Morning and Evening Prayer'. As the titles suggest, the first provides the full version of Morning Prayer and Evening Prayer, just as they are found in the 'Divine Office', while the latter is less comprehensive: it does cover the standard Morning Prayer and Evening Prayer – as well as Night Prayer – but offers only a selection of the material that the fuller versions provide. At this stage any of the four office-books would serve your purpose, though it might be advisable to begin with one or other of the shorter versions, which of course are much less expensive than the 'Divine Office'. One thing is certain: once you have become accustomed to praying Morning Prayer and Evening Prayer, you should not have much trouble in branching out further and discovering for yourself more of the treasures that the Office has to offer.

A final practical point: before launching into Morning Prayer or Evening Prayer for the first time, you would be well advised to spend a little time in familiarising yourself with the book you are going to use, preferably, as has already been mentioned, with the help of a knowledgeable friend or fellow-parishioner: read through its table of contents, flip through its pages, note how the Office is arranged over four weeks (so that there are references to Week One, Week Two, Week Three and Week Four), find out where various items, such as the hymns or the Gospel Canticles, are located. Such a brief familiarisation will enable you to use the office-book with confidence and, what is infinitely more important, to concentrate all your attention not on the book but on the praying of the Prayer of the Church.

A Postscript

So far it has been the essentials of Morning Prayer and Evening Prayer that have been presented. Now a few further clarifications may be added:

Introduction: The appeal for God's help at the beginning of Morning Prayer and Evening Prayer is made up of a versicle (or brief verse, indicated by V/): 'O God, come to our aid' and a response (indicated by R/): 'O Lord, make haste to help us', and ends with the 'Glory be to the Father', followed (except in Lent) by 'Alleluia'.

You may be puzzled by references to the 'Invitatory' (pronounced Invitatory); it is simply a more elaborate Introduction for the Office of the day. It need not be used by those who pray only Morning Prayer and Evening Prayer, though it is not without its attractiveness and is well worth using at least from time to time. Like the usual introduction, the Invitatory begins with a versicle (in this case, 'Lord, open our lips', accompanied by a sign of the cross on the lips), and the response: 'And we shall praise your name.' But – and this gives it its special charm – it also includes Psalm 94, a majestic song of praise, which invites us to come into the presence of God, our Creator King, with joy and thanksgiving in our hearts; to bow down and bend low before him; at the same time it reminds us to 'listen to his voice'. As Jesus taught, it isn't enough to simply mouth words, to say 'Lord, Lord'; we must also do the will of the Lord: the praying of the Office is suspect if it does not affect the way we live. (For the sake of variety, Psalm 94 may be replaced by Psalm 24, 66 or 99).

The Psalms: The GI suggests three possible ways in which the psalms may be said or sung (*cf §121*): either the whole psalm is sung by everyone; or two sections of the congregation take alternate verses; or it is sung responsorially, an antiphon being repeated by everyone after each verse, as with the responsorial psalm at Mass. However, in presenting these three ways of praying the psalms, the GI is not excluding others; for example, it can be most effective on some occasions to have a solo voice reading or singing the whole psalm, or picking out words obviously meant to be the words of God (e.g. Psalm 45:11: 'Be still and know that I am God...'). Other psalms, such as 14 ('Lord, who shall be admitted to your tent...?') or 23 ('The Lord's is the earth and its fullness') easily lend themselves to a more imaginative approach.

This diagram shows a typical page from Evening Prayer.

Antiphon

Title giving the general sense of the psalm as originally intended

A brief suggestion of how the psalm can be interpreted in a Christian sense

The number of the psalm. The number in brackets gives the Hebrew enumeration.

The numerals I and II indicate that a longer psalm has been divided in two.

The psalm is presented in verse-form, as in a poem

The 'Glory be to the Father' is added to the end of each psalm.

PSALMODY

Ant.I: The Lord is my light and my help; whom shall I fear?†

Eastertide: God has exalted him at his own right hand as leader and Saviour, alleluia.

TRUST IN TIME OF AFFLICTION — PSALM 26(27)

Behold, the place where God dwells among men (Rev 21:3)

I

The Lord is my light and my help;*
whom shall I fear?
The Lord is the stronghold of my life;*
before whom shall I shrink?

When evil-doers draw near*
to devour my flesh,
it is they, my enemies and foes,*
who stumble and fall.

Though an army encamp against me*
my heart would not fear.
Though war break out against me*
even then would I trust.

There is one thing I ask of the Lord,*
for this I long,
to live in the house of the Lord,*
all the days of my life,
to savour the sweetness of the Lord,*
to behold his temple.

For there he keeps me safe in his tent*
in the day of evil.
He hides me in the shelter of his tent,*
on a rock he sets me safe.

And now my head shall be raised*
above my foes who surround me
and I shall offer within his tent
a sacrifice of joy.*
I will sing and make music for the Lord.

Ant. The Lord is my light and my help; whom shall I fear?
Eastertide: God has exalted him at his own right hand as leader and Saviour, alleluia.

Each psalm (and canticle) has its Antiphon, which is recited immediately before (and may be repeated after) the psalm itself. Its purpose is to highlight the theme of the psalm or emphasise some aspect of it, usually by singling out a key verse from the psalm itself. However, it may also be used to suggest how this or that psalm can be linked with a specific season (Eastertide, for example) or with a special festival (such as the feast of the Body and Blood of Christ). When, as in the psalm illustrated, the first Antiphon is identical with the psalm's opening words, it is followed by a 'dagger' to show that the identical words need not be repeated.

In addition to the Antiphon, there are two 'Titles', which appear at the head of each psalm. Like the Antiphons, they are offered as a possible help to our prayer and so should be used only in the measure that we find them useful. The first presents a brief description of the original sense of the psalm, while the second, taken from the New Testament or an early Christian writer, illustrates how the psalm may be given a specifically Christian slant. Thus, in the psalm illustrated, the first 'title' tells us that the psalm is about 'Trust in time of affliction', and the second provides a scripture reference from the book of Revelation. In private recitation the second title may be used in place of the antiphon (*GI§11*).

The 'Glory be to the Father' comes at the end of each psalm, but where one long psalm is divided in two, as in the illustration, it can be prayed as one single psalm without interruption, in which case, the 'Glory be to the Father' at the end of the first section and the Antiphon at the beginning of the second are omitted.

References

1. B Hume *Searching for God* Hodder & Stoughton, London (1977) p51

2. Thomas Merton *The Psalms are our Prayers* Burns and Oates, London (1957) p20

3. Another example of greater flexibility is to be found in the GI's attitude towards those, such as clerics, who have the duty of saying the whole Office each day. While in no sense downgrading that duty, it speaks of it in terms of the vital need of the Church rather than of mere legal obligation. Furthermore, it recognises the differing importance of the various hours, from Morning and Evening Prayer which 'should not be omitted except for a serious reason' to the Office of Readings which is 'a liturgical celebration of the word of God' and therefore particularly important for those who have to preach the word to others, to Prayer during the Day and Night Prayers 'in order to sanctify the whole day more completely ... (and) to round off the whole Opus Dei and to commend themselves to God before retiring' (*§29*).

4. *Directory on Sunday Celebrations in the absence of a priest* §33

5. See *The Tablet* March 1992, p306

4 – Psalms in the Prayer of the Church

'That delightful book, the book of the psalms' (St Ambrose)

'The reason why the Church loves the Psalms ... is not merely that they have been sent to her by God ...but because God has given himself to her in them, as though in a sacrament.' (Thomas Merton)[1]

The Psalms hold a unique place in the Prayer of the Church: without them, it would simply cease to be. They are like the flesh that clothes the skeleton or, better still, the heart that enlivens the frame. That is why Vatican II urged all who pray the Divine Office to 'take steps to improve their understanding of the liturgy and of the bible, especially of the psalms (*CL§90; underlining added*). There can be no doubt that the Holy Spirit will always be present with us when we use these 'magnificent songs' in a spirit of faith and love, but his presence does not smooth away all problems. We can still 'sometimes experience difficulties in making this inspired prayer our own' (*GI§101*), and so we are left with the task of deepening our understanding according to our abilities and opportunities. The purpose of this chapter is to help in that task by offering background information about the psalms, highlighting their principal features and suggesting how these inspired, pre-Christian poems may be used as Christian prayer.

Prayers with a Pedigree

Some years ago a national newspaper carried a small but intriguing heading. 'World's oldest book is unveiled', it proclaimed. Beneath was the story of how an exhibition hosted by the Egyptian antiquities organisation had put on display some well-thumbed parchment pages, all bound together between wooden covers; how this book, the most ancient of its kind in existence, was reckoned to be sixteen hundred years old; how its contents consisted of a complete copy of the book of psalms; and how it had been found in a coffin in Egypt, placed under the head of a little girl. It is an amazing thought that just about the time when Anglo-Saxon tribesmen were beginning to occupy this country, a youngster was praying the psalms in far-away Egypt. Presumably she had a special affection for them; was not that why her parents had ensured that the psalter should be placed in her coffin with her? And yet, even sixteen hundred years ago, there was nothing new in a person praying the psalms: countless Christian men and women had already done so. And long before the birth of Jesus the psalter was already established as the prayer book of the Jews. (The lady who blissfully expressed her delight that even the Jews used the psalms, knew little of the psalter's history!) Many of the psalms date back 3,000 years; some are even older.

How, then, have they managed to appeal to so many people over so long a period – no other prayer book can remotely compare with them in this respect – and how is it that they still remain at the heart of Christian prayer today? Why should prayers that were composed so long ago by people so different from ourselves in so many ways – in culture, in attitude, in language, in ways of expression – still interest us?

I believe one answer must be that the psalms strike a chord deep in the human heart. For 'though the psalms originated very many centuries ago among an Eastern people, they express the pain and hope, the unhappiness and trust of people of every age and country, and sing above all of faith in God, of revelation and of redemption' (*GI§107*). A rabbi has recounted how one of his friends was serving in a tank corps during the Arab-Israeli October War. In a rapidly deteriorating situation he picked up his Hebrew Bible and sought comfort in reading the psalms aloud, though very quietly. However it was not quietly enough: his words were picked up on the intercom and some of his colleagues, who would have called themselves 'secular' rather than believing Jews, asked him what he was reading. Rather sheepishly he explained that it was the psalms and, to his astonishment, heard the reply: 'Well, don't keep them to yourself, then!' – and of course he didn't[2]. The psalms reflect the humanity that is shared by the men and women of all times and places. Their outpourings of praise for God and their pleas for his help are not foreign to anyone who strives to pray, and their transparent honesty – their readiness to 'tell it as it is', and even to call God's action (or inaction) into question on occasion – has an appealing charm about it. But perhaps the most impressive feature is the powerful faith which undergirds them and is the source from which they well up; their authors have no doubt about God's existence or his power or his concern for them. It is a deep, rock-like faith, yet a faith all the more remarkable in view of the fact that, as we shall see, the psalmists did not believe in an after-life, at least not in the way we understand it. It seems almost incredible that with at best a limited comprehension of God's plans for their eternal future, they should still have been able to produce prayers of such splendid calibre.

However, there is a more momentous reason why the psalms hold a prime position in the prayer of the Church: the book of the psalms is a biblical book, and that means that, like any other book of the bible, it is inspired. It is not simply the work of human beings; though it is written by them and betrays their own characteristic styles and outlooks and limitations, yet the One ultimately responsible for it is God himself. In the words of a famous French scholar, it took God to provide prayers worthy of himself. The psalter therefore stands alone as a divinely inspired prayer book. Furthermore, it holds the unique privilege of being the prayer book used by Jesus himself, by our Lady, by the apostles, by St Paul. These were the prayers that the Lord learned at his mother's knee; these were the prayers that accompanied him all his life through. He would have prayed some of them every day of his life. In all his recorded sayings, he quotes them more often than any other part of the Old Testament, and they were on his lips at the end. He prayed them with his friends before leaving the Upper Room to go to the Garden of Gethsemane and from there to his death, and, even as he hung dying on the cross, prayed them still: "My God, my God, why have you forsaken me?" (*Psalm 21)*; "Father, into your hands I commend my spirit" (*Psalm 30*). In praying the psalms we are literally praying Jesus' own prayers. And so Thomas Merton could write that: 'Together with the Our Father, which Jesus himself gave us, the Psalms are in the most perfect sense the "prayer of Jesus" '[3].

The Psalms in Perspective

The psalms have a pedigree beyond compare, and on that account alone deserve to be incorporated into our prayers; but they will not yield their full potential as prayers until we make them our own, until we discover their value for ourselves. As a first step, however, we need to try and understand what they meant to the psalmists who composed them and to their contemporaries who were the first to sing them. We need to try and get into their hearts and minds, see things from their point of view. It will help us to enter into the outlook of that ancient world in which the psalmists lived if we familiarise ourselves with some of its key concepts:

<u>After-life:</u> During most of the period covered by the Old Testament the Hebrew people believed that after death everyone, whether good or bad, descends into Sheol, a desolate under-world abode where they live a shadowy existence; it is not real life, for there they are not even able to praise God. Because Sheol is only a kind of half-living, the term is frequently used in the psalms metaphorically to express any kind of distress, such as sickness or persecution; for example: 'Out of the depths (literally, Sheol) I cry to you, O Lord' (*Psalm 139*). Though some of the psalms seem already to point in this direction (see, for example, the last verses of Psalm 15 in *Evening Prayer, Sunday, Week 2*), only later did notions of reward and punishment and bodily resurrection surface explicitly. It is easy to understand how before that, it seemed imperative that justice should be done (and be seen to be done) in this life, a consideration to be borne in mind in dealing with psalms that speak of vengeance. Again, their limited understanding of life beyond the grave helps to explain why in their psalms the Hebrew people often prayed for temporal benefits, such as food and wine or a large and prosperous family.

<u>Covenant:</u> A key notion in the Old Testament is that God entered a unique relationship with the Hebrew people on mount Sinai. The prophet Jeremiah summarises what this means when he 'speaks on the Lord's behalf' the words: 'I will be their God and they will be my people' (*31:33*). God

undertakes to care for them and protect them as a prize possession, while they, on their part, must respond by obedience. Whatever the purpose of a particular psalm (whether it be praise, thanksgiving or petition) its underlying motivation is always the covenant; it is because of God's truth (utter faithfulness) and loving-kindness, two typical aspects of the covenant relationship, that God can be praised and pleaded with. And even when things go badly awry and it looks as though they have been forgotten, the people know they can still jog God's memory by appealing to the covenant, to that very special relationship between God and themselves. However, like any other relationship, the covenant is a dynamic not a static reality; it is in the living out of the relationship that the people come to an ever clearer understanding of their God.

God: The psalmists speak to God rather than about God; what they offer is prayer, not theology. Nonetheless, a theology does peep through what they write. It is clear that in earlier times they, like the peoples round about them, accepted that each of the nations had its own god or gods, though they believed that Israel's God was in every way superior to the others. Thus, in Psalm 94 ('Come, ring out your joy to the Lord') the God of Israel is described as 'a great king above all gods'. There was only a short step between seeing other gods as lesser deities, mere citizens of the great King God, and seeing them as 'nothings'; however, it was only after a lengthy period of development that Israel finally arrived at the belief that there is, and can be, only one God and that this one God alone is to be worshipped. Once this stage is reached ridicule is heaped upon the powerless, so-called gods of the pagans, who have eyes but cannot see, ears and cannot hear, and so on. (*See the latter part of Psalm 134* ['Praise the name of the Lord'] *in Evening Prayer, Friday, Week Three.)*

Jerusalem: No city meant so much to Israel as did Jerusalem, not simply because it was the capital of the country, but because it was 'the city of God', 'his holy mountain', God's special dwelling place in their midst, and they loved 'her very stones' (*Psalm 101*). It was in Jerusalem that their intense monotheistic faith was most clearly manifested: the magnificent Temple (see below), built by Solomon, witnessed solemn liturgies in all their splendour, with music, singing and dance, with processions and sacrifices and richly embroidered vestments. It seems more than likely that most of the psalms were composed precisely for this setting. Three times each year all adult males were expected to go up to Jerusalem – it was built on a hill-top almost two and a half thousand feet above sea level – to celebrate the great feasts of Passover, Pentecost and Tabernacles. Originally agricultural festivals, the feasts came to be linked with the three towering events of Israel's history – deliverance from slavery in Egypt, the making of the covenant and the giving of the Law on Mount Sinai, and the forty years of wandering in the desert when they were forged into a people. It is hardly surprising that Jerusalem ('city of shalom [peace]', according to popular interpretation), usually under the alternative name of Sion[4], appears time and again in the psalms; indeed, some psalms are so centred upon the city that they are commonly referred to as 'Sion Songs'. (*Psalm 136* ['By the rivers of Babylon'] shows how grieved the people of Israel were when their Babylonian captors taunted them with the words: 'Sing to us ... one of Sion's songs'). High emotions filled the hearts of the people at the thought of going on pilgrimage to Jerusalem, going, as they put it, 'to see the face of God'. ('I rejoiced when I heard them say: "Let us go to God's house" ' [*Psalm 122; see Evening Prayer, Monday, Week Three]*), but equally they were distraught with anguish when Jerusalem was laid waste in the sixth century B.C.

<u>Law:</u> For the Hebrews the word 'Law' (Torah) had not the exclusively legalistic connotation it has for us. It meant not so much rules and regulations as 'instruction' or 'guidance'. The first five books of the Old Testament were called 'the Law', though they are concerned primarily not with commandments but with the whole of God's dealings with his people during the foundational period of their history. This suggests that the people's experience of what God had done for them was both a revelation of God's loving concern and also an 'instruction', an indication of the kind of lives expected of them in return. Some scholars speak of the morality of the Bible as 'remembrance morality': 'Remember what God has done for you in bringing you out of Egypt, in giving you freedom etc, and then behave accordingly.' Thus, Law is instruction as to how the whole of

one's life can be lived in harmony with the covenant. (Looking at it from a Christian perspective, we might translate the word 'law' in the psalms as 'gospel living'.) Law was a blessing from God, something in which the psalmists rejoiced. The first psalm, which in some sense sets the tone for the rest, ponders on the contrasting fate that befalls those who respect the law and those who reject it. In succeeding psalms the word 'law' appears times without number, reaching a climax in Psalm 118, the longest psalm in the whole psalter, which from beginning to end focuses upon the law, either explicitly or under one of seven synonyms: word, promise, command, statute, decree, precept or will. This psalm (which runs to no less than one hundred and seventy-six verses!) worms its way through the monthly cycle of the Prayer of the Church: it has been divided into twenty-two sections and scarcely a day goes by when at least one of those sections is not recited at one or other of the Hours. Its overall theme can be summed up in words taken from the psalm itself: 'Lord, how I love your law.' We are able to love God's law because, as Israel understood, obedience to that law far from robbing us of our freedom actually set us free to respond fittingly to a God whose loving kindness has been revealed to us and whose desire is that we should be fully human.

Name: The term '(God's) name' appears more than one hundred and fifty times in the course of the psalms. We have only to listen to the way the psalmists speak of it – as something to be trusted, praised, given thanks to, rejoiced in, greeted with the song of psalms – to realise that it has personal overtones. To the Shakespearian question: 'What's in a name?', I suspect that the psalmists would have answered firmly: 'Everything'. For them and their people, a name – the name of anyone, but above all the name of God – was more than a distinctive tag; it was a revelation of that person's nature and power, in some strange way it was identified with the individual him or herself. Exodus 3:13-15 tells of one of the crucial events in the life of Moses: the revelation to him of the divine name, a mysterious name which scholars think was probably pronounced *Yahweh*. It was judged to be so sacred, so filled with power, that eventually the people would no longer take it on their lips but substituted for it the word 'Lord'. It was in fact spoken aloud, though in a whisper, just once per year: in the holiest place (the Holy of Holies: see below under 'Temple'), on one of the holiest of days (the Day of Atonement), by the – officially – holiest member of the community (the High Priest). And so when we pray, for example, Psalm 8 (*see Morning Prayer, Saturday, Week Two*), which is framed by the exclamation 'How great is your name, O Lord our God, through all the earth', we do well to recall that in extolling the awesome name of God we are extolling God himself in all his power and glory and majesty.

Preferential Option for the Poor: These words are no where to be found in the psalter, yet what they imply is present everywhere. That explains at least in part why the psalms are so dear to oppressed people in the Third World – and beyond. The psalmists present to us a God who 'stoops down' in compassionate concern for the poor, the afflicted, the needy, the lowly; who is father to orphans and husband to widows; who 'from the dust ... lifts up the lowly, from the dungheap raises the poor' (*Psalm 112; see Evening Prayer, Saturday, Week Two*). And he promises a special blessing to those who show the same concern for the poor and needy:

'Happy the man who considers the poor and the weak.
The Lord will save him in the day of evil,
will guard him, give him life, make him happy in the land'
(*Psalm 40; see Friday, Evening Prayer, Week One*).

Walter Brueggemann, one of today's finest commentators on the psalms, notes that 'Israel's prayer life ... is saturated with the issue of justice'[5]. Similarly, he writes that 'Religious hungers in Israel never preclude justice questions'[6]. It may be impossible to pinpoint the precise identity of the 'enemies' and 'oppressors' whom we hear so much about in the psalms, but that doesn't matter. We know that ancient Israel was surrounded by the superpowers of its day and its people suffered much at their hands: death squads and secret police – or their ancient equivalents – were not unknown to Israel. God's people experienced exile and the hopelessness that so many refugees experience today, while, again as in our day, some suffered injustice and exploitation even at the hand of domestic oppressors. It is little wonder that the God of Israel is so often called upon as a God of battles, as their only defender and only hope. To pray the psalms is – or should be – to become more sensitive to the concerns of all people who are oppressed, humiliated or driven from their homes.

Temple: It was King Solomon, David's son, who built the first Temple in Jerusalem, taking seven years to complete the task.

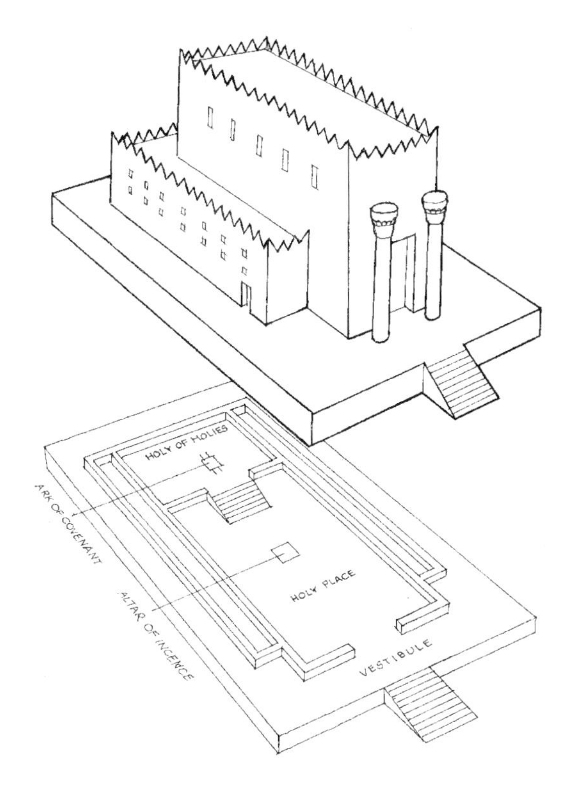

By today's standards it was not a large building, more the size of a parish church than that of a cathedral (about 90 x 30 feet, and with its plinth standing some 55 feet high), though it was probably the largest Israelite construction up to that time. It consisted of three sections: first, a short vestibule, then the largest part called the Holy Place and finally the most sacred part of all – the smaller square room known as the Holy of Holies. While recognising that God's real home is in heaven, Israel viewed the Temple as his dwelling place in their midst – 'The Lord is in his holy temple, the Lord, whose throne is in heaven' (Psalm 10:4). Furthermore, the Temple stood as a sign of God's special choice of Israel and of the city of Jerusalem, as well as serving as the 'stage' for Israel's worship, including the singing of the psalms with their accompanying music. It held a unique place in the affection of the people – and of the psalmists. 'How lovely is your dwelling place, Lord, God of hosts' sang one of them. 'My soul is longing and yearning, is yearning for the courts of the Lord' (Psalm 83:3).

Hence the devastating grief when at the beginning of the 6th century Jerusalem fell to the Babylonians and the Temple was reduced to a heap of rubble. At the end of the exile some of the people returned from Babylon to their own land and eventually built another Temple. In the life time of that Temple the collection of psalms, eventually assuming its final form, continued to play a central role in the liturgy, which is why the psalter can justifiably be called 'The Prayer Book of the Second Temple'.

The Universe: By our standards, the cosmology of the psalms may seem primitive, but then in their songs of praise the psalmists are not attempting to teach science; they are inviting us to worship with them the mighty God who brought the universe into existence and keeps it there. They speak of the effortless way in which he creates: he simply commands and things are. 'By his word the heavens were made, by the breath of his mouth all the stars' (*Psalm 32; see Morning Prayer, Tuesday, Week One*). Creation stories which were widespread in the ancient Near East pictured God having to conquer fearsome dark waters before he was able to begin the work of creation; and even then the danger always remained that they might sweep back and undo creation. The notion must have lingered in the minds of the Israelites because in some of their psalms they refer to the 'waters' as though they were a threatening enemy – indeed, they sometimes speak of them as though they were live creatures; for example, as 'Leviathan' (*Psalm 73:14*) or 'Rahab' (*Psalm 88:10f*) – but the significant thing is that God has no difficulty in taming them:

'The waters have lifted up, O Lord,
The waters have lifted up their voice,
The water have lifted up their thunder.

Greater than the roar of mighty waters,
more glorious than the surgings of the sea,
the Lord is glorious on high'
(*Psalm 92: see Morning Prayer, Sunday, Week Three*).

If we try to visualise, through the mentality of the people of Israel, the universe which God had made and in which they his special creatures lived, then it would look something like this:

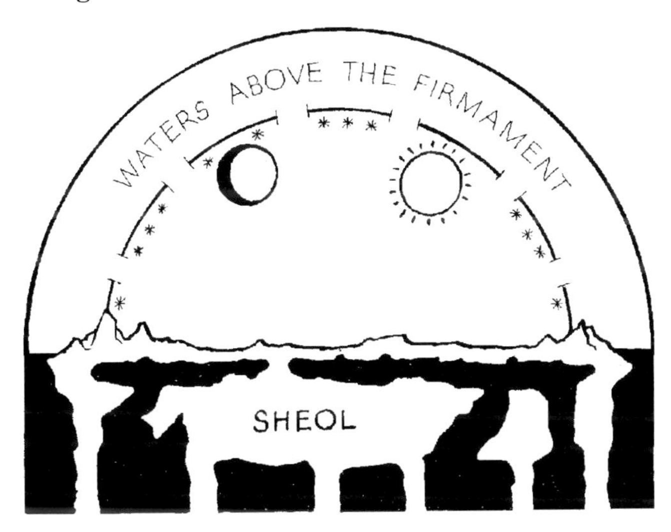

The earth itself is flat, poised above the 'waters below' and upheld by pillars. At the ends of the earth there are mountains to support the firmament, which might be compared to an upturned basin, a solid vault to which the heavenly bodies – sun, moon and stars – are attached and which holds back the 'waters above'. This firmament is pierced by windows which are opened to let the rain fall upon the earth beneath. Way above the upper waters is the home of God himself; and under the earth, apparently below the nether waters, lies Sheol. (The waters surrounding the universe above and below doubtless refer to the idea, mentioned above, of fearsome waters that had to be displaced by God to make room for the world.)

The Psalms in History

It will also be a help to our understanding of the psalms if, in addition to these key concepts, we keep in mind at least a skeleton outline of Israel's history, for the psalms are a product of that history, inevitably coloured by it and their meaning often illuminated by it. We might picture four volumes, each one covering roughly 500 years, so that together they stretch from 2000 BC to the birth of Christ, and each volume named after a representative person or event.

So, volume one, which covers the period 2000 to 1500BC, is entitled: ABRAHAM. Here we meet the 'father' of God's people. About 1850BC, Abraham leaves his own country (modern Iraq), and, together with his wife and flocks, sets out for a land which, he believes, God will show him. The land turns out to be Canaan (what we now know as Palestine/Israel), a strip of land bordering the Mediterranean Sea. There God enters into a covenant with him, promising that one day he will have the land as his own, a great nation will spring from him and ultimately in him all nations will be blessed. Centuries later the psalmist will sing:

'The princes of the peoples (i.e. the Gentiles) are assembled
with the people of Abraham's God' (*46:10*).
(*See Morning Prayer, Wednesday, Week One*)

The promises are kept alive through his sons Isaac and Jacob, and through the latter's twelve sons, especially Joseph. As his father's favourite, he earns the jealousy of his brothers who sell him as a slave to Ishmaelites on their way to Egypt. There he prospers, becoming second only to the Pharaoh in prestige and power; and so, when famine strikes Canaan, he is able to offer hospitality to his brothers and their families, and the assurance of Pharaoh's protection. For a long time they flourish, but then ...

And so to volume two, 1500-1000BC: MOSES. As the Hebrews grow in numbers the Egyptians see them as a threat; fear turns to open persecution, forced labour and finally murder of male Hebrew children at birth. Moses, having only narrowly escaped that fate, eventually emerges as the charismatic leader of his people. He is unquestionably one of the towering figures in the Old Testament; to him the name of God is revealed, and his unwavering faith, his keen insight into God's plans and his ability to galvanise the people into action, make him, humanly speaking, their saviour. He leads them forth from slavery in Egypt, across the Sea of Reeds, and into freedom. This escape, the Exodus, is the key event in Israel's history, the foundation of their faith and their religion, the date when Israel came to birth as a nation. It proved not only that God had chosen them but also that he had power to protect them against even the most formidable enemy, for it was he, rather than Moses, who had led them with outstretched arm and power in his hand. At mount Sinai in the desert he enters into solemn covenant with them and delivers the ten commandments, the sign that much is expected of those who are God's 'peculiar people'; they must live in keeping with the special relationship. After years of wandering in the desert and shortly after Moses' death, they come within sight of the Promised Land. But only gradually, in the course of a couple of centuries, will they infiltrate and finally make it their own.

The third volume, 1000-500BC, belongs to DAVID. As the people settled in Canaan, so they had to face enemies from many quarters. At first it was the 'Judges' (warlords, we might call them) who rose to their defence, but in the end the people got what they wanted – a king of their own. The greatest of their kings was David. Under him and his son Solomon, Israel enjoyed a golden age, or so it seemed in retrospect. He extended Israel's borders; defeated its ancient enemy, the Philistines; united the twelve tribes, the descendants of Jacob's sons, to a degree that had never before been possible; and captured Jerusalem, making it his capital and enshrining there as a symbol of God's presence the Ark of the Covenant, a portable box in which the stone tablets of the ten commandments were kept. The country witnessed prosperity, the growth of a fitting temple liturgy, and an eruption of literary activity. Among the fruit of the latter were many, if not most, of the psalms. Success, however, was short-lived: with the death of Solomon, the tribes began to drift apart, finally dividing into two separate kingdoms, the northern one of Israel, with its capital in Samaria, and the southern one of Judah which retained its capital in Jerusalem. Weakened, deaf to the prophets who called them to repentance, and led for the most part by inadequate rulers, both kingdoms became a prey to other powerful nations; the northern kingdom succumbed to the Assyrians (inhabitants of present day Iraq) towards the end of the eighth century, and within one hundred and fifty years a similar fate befell the kingdom of Judah at the hands of the Babylonians, who had succeeded to the empire of the Assyrians.

The final volume, 500 to the time of Christ[7], has the name not of a person but of an event – the EXILE. It was the most traumatic crisis in the long history of the people of God. Their city, God's own city, together with its Temple was laid in ruins and the king and his people taken into exile. But the fifty years of Exile were to prove a time of purification in which the people discovered anew both their God and themselves, and the absolute value of the bond between them. They had no Temple, no king, no sacrifices, but they still could, and still did, worship him. They began to value their written records as never before: most of the books that make up the Old Testament, including the psalter itself, achieved their present form either during the exile or in the years that followed. Eventually under the patronage of the all-conquering Persians, the exiles were set free and allowed to return home, but the threat from other superpowers was far from over: Palestine was to fall under the control of the Greeks in the fourth century BC and of the Romans in the first. But throughout all the upheavals, Israel retained its faith in God, and increasingly its hopes that he would bring about a new world, centred upon a 'Messiah'. Their hopes were not misplaced, for in fact at the end of this period came the day when the whole of the history outlined above, and the psalter itself, was about to find its fulfilment: Jesus Christ was born in Bethlehem.

'Poems of Praise'

Some years ago a group of 'difficult' children was taken on holiday to Wales by two nuns and a school chaplain. Since they planned to do some hill-walking, the youngsters were all suitably kitted out. One of them, soon to prove the problem character of the party, could not be separated from her bright orange cagoule – it was even rumoured that she wore it in bed! One morning, as the Sisters and the priest were praying Morning Prayer, they became aware of someone in the kitchen doorway. That orange-clad figure could only be, to give her the nickname she had already acquired, 'Orange Blossom'. Contrary to expectations, she was not about to cause mayhem. She simply stood there in silence until the breviaries were finally closed, and then she announced: 'I liked that; it was poetry, wasn't it?' (She liked it so much that each morning thereafter she was to be found sitting in the midst of the group as they prayed Morning Prayer.)

'It was poetry, wasn't it?' Orange Blossom had discovered for herself what the GI expresses more formally: that 'the psalms are not readings or prose... but poems of praise' (*GI§102*). The youngster had been able to sense that, despite the absence of rhyme and discernible metre, the psalms and canticles are real poetry; she could tell that they had movement, a lilt, a rhythm about them. In the main these effects are achieved by a very simple device, which an 18th century Anglican bishop aptly described as 'parallelism': the psalmist repeats the same thought in succeeding lines.

Sometimes the parallel lines say much the same thing but in different words; they match each other like a pair of gloves!

'On my bed I remember you,
on you I muse through the night' (*Psalm 62:7*).
Or: 'The heavens proclaim the glory of God
and the firmament shows forth the work of his hands'
(*Psalm 18:2*).

At other times a similar result is obtained by the use of contrasting ideas: the lines correspond to each other like the 'heads' and 'tails' of the same coin:

'The Lord raises the lowly;
he humbles the wicked to the dust' (*Psalm 146:6*).
Or: 'They will collapse and fall
but we shall hold and stand firm' (*Psalm 19:9*).

On yet other occasions the first line is developed or filled out by the parallel line (or lines): they complement or 'complete' each other like a happily married couple:

'He is my love, my fortress;
he is my stronghold, my saviour,
my shield, my place of refuge' (*Psalm 143*).
Or: 'they (the just) will flourish in the courts of the Lord
still bearing fruit when they are old,
still full of sap, still green,
to proclaim that the Lord is just' (*Psalm 91*).

Like western poetry, the poetry of the Hebrews also achieves its effects by adopting such devices as word-play, refrains, alliteration and so forth. But parallelism, often appearing in more complex patterns than those just described, is still its most notable feature. And that is particularly fortunate for us who read the psalms not in their original language but in translation. As C S Lewis shrewdly noted: 'It is ... either a wonderful piece of luck or a wise provision of God's, that poetry which was to be turned into all languages should have as its chief formal characteristic one that does not disappear ... (even) in translation'[8], i.e. parallelism. Thus the whole human race can respond to the invitation to sing the psalms 'to the glory of his name'. It is also worth noting that parallelism makes it easier to linger over a sentiment that is attractively presented in the psalms.

However, poetry has other striking features – it uses metaphors and symbols, it gives free rein to the emotions, it is often allusive and sometimes seems to strain human language to its limits. How important that we recognise all this when we turn to the psalms, for 'Where but in poetry can "mountains skip like rams and hills like lambs" (*Psalm 113:4,6*)? Where but in poetry could it be imagined that "the meadows clothe themselves with flocks, the valleys deck themselves with grain, they shout and sing together for joy" (*Psalm 64:13*)? Where but in poetry can a male become pregnant: "Behold, the wicked man conceives evil, and is pregnant with mischief, and brings forth lies (*Psalm 7:14*)?"... Indeed, where but in poetry can any language for God be found?'[9]. God appears in the poetry of the psalms in all manner of guises: not only is he father and, at least by implication, mother, and shepherd and king and judge, but also rock and fortress and light and shield and water. Though the psalmists speak in wonder of his greatness and magnificence, they are not afraid to speak about him, and even to him, in a way that most of us would hardly dare. For example: 'Awake, Lord, why do you sleep', and even 'Then the Lord awoke ... like a warrior overcome with wine' (*Psalm 77:65*)! They describe him in homely terms as scanning with his eyes, hearing with his ears, stretching out his hand to hold us tight in a world where evil often seems to prosper; he covers us with the shadow of his wings – like a mother hen – and his face lights up with a smile, a smile that spells our happiness.

Poems can be placed in different categories – sonnets, odes, ballads, epics and so on – and so too can the psalms. This is fortunate, for it means that once we are familiar with the style and structure of a particular category – its 'family traits', if you like – then it's going to be easier for us to spot other psalms of the same family, and, broadly speaking, we shall know what to expect of them. Of course even within a family the various members are not clones of each other: each is special, unrepeatable. Similarly, each of the psalms is unique and therefore ideally we should study each one on its own, but, since such a study is well beyond the scope of this book, it is all the more important that we have an overall view of the main families[10]. In fact there are just two main ones, reflecting the two poles of life: its joys and its griefs, its happiness and its sorrow. They are psalms of praise and psalms of petition.

1. Psalms of Praise

The normal pattern for these psalms, usually called 'hymns', is simple. It begins with a brief summons to praise the Lord, which may be directed to the people ('Praise, O servants of the Lord' [*Psalm 112*]), to the whole world ('Praise the Lord, all you nations' [*Psalm 116*]), or even to the psalmist himself ('Bless the Lord, my soul' [*Psalm 103*]). Then comes the main body of the psalm, giving reasons for the praise; they are almost invariably God's creative and/or redemptive work. Finally, often though not always, the summons to praise is repeated. Thus, Psalm 116 (*Morning Prayer, Saturday, Week Three*), the shortest psalm in the psalter, is a typical hymn:

'O praise the Lord, all you nations,
acclaim him, all you peoples (Summons).

Strong is his love for us.
He is faithful for ever'(Motivation).

Within the general category of hymns, there are several sub-groups, each of them consisting of a number of psalms which share a common concern. Thus, there are the half-dozen 'enthronement' psalms, which praise God for his kingship ('The Lord is king, let earth rejoice' [*Psalm 96*]); another half-dozen 'Sion Songs', which praise him in his holy city ('The Lord is great and worthy to be praised/ in the city of our God' [*Psalm 47*]). And there are also 'thanksgiving' psalms, which praise God for favours received ('It is good to give thanks to the Lord' [*Psalm 91*]). The Hebrew word for 'thanks' or 'thanksgiving' (*todah*) can equally well be translated as 'praise'; so it's hardly surprising that thanksgiving psalms are also classed as psalms of praise.

2. Psalms of Petition

These psalms, which make up about 40% of the psalter, follow a more complex pattern than the psalms of praise. They are pleas, sometimes desperate pleas, for help, because the psalmist and/or the community face some danger or difficulty or crisis. They usually include some or all of the following elements, though not necessarily in this order:

i) an initial cry to the Lord, such as 'To my words give ear, O Lord' (*Psalm 5:2*), or 'Help, O Lord, for good men have vanished' (*Psalm 11:2*);

ii) reasons for the cry, usually taking the form of a vivid account of the psalmist's plight. Though bold imagery is used, it is often so vague that the precise nature of the trouble is left unclear. However, this lack of clarity has the benefit of making these psalms suitable for all kinds of situations, beyond that in the mind of the psalmist;

iii) repeated expressions of trust in God;

iv) a petition for help, often giving reasons (sometimes very bold ones) why God should intervene, and at times accompanied by expressions of vindictiveness which may shock us (about which, more in a moment);

v) finally, there is often an unexpected change of mood; it's perhaps because the psalmist's faith has been deepened by the prayer, or perhaps because the prayer takes place after the event (it is in the form of a flashback), or perhaps because one of the temple priests or prophets has given an assurance that the prayer will be heard; in any event, plea gives way to praise. Sometimes there is a promise to fulfil vows that have been made or to offer a sacrifice.

Other psalms might be gathered under this heading because they express that trust in God which is one of the striking features of psalms of petition [*see iii) above*]. They usually begin with an expression of trust and confidence, and simply go on to enlarge upon it throughout the rest of the prayer. They are known as psalms of trust and they are among the most attractive in the psalter; Psalm 22, for example ('The Lord is my Shepherd'), is among them.

However, as has been pointed out, psalms of petition can disturb us, particularly when pleas for help are accompanied by intemperate language, vindictiveness, a thirst for revenge. Indeed, three complete psalms, as well as verses from several others, have been omitted from the Prayer of the Church on that account (*GI§131*). But what of the 'un-Christian' sentiments that remain? Firstly, ancient Semitic people went in for language which we might describe as 'over the top': they both praised and cursed with gusto! Nor did they appreciate the distinction between hating the sin and hating the sinner which we take for granted. Moreover, the raw emotions so evident in the psalms are present in us all, even though we may be reluctant to own them. When a psalm seems 'offensive', it is good to ask: who could possibly need to pray a psalm like that today? And the answer might be: a woman who has just been brutally raped, or a parent whose child has been mowed down by a drunken driver: these people know all about seething rage and desire for the punishment of a wrongdoer. In praying the Prayer of the Church are we not embracing such people in our prayer? Secondly, lacking a clear understanding of reward and punishment in an after-life, the psalmists believe that God must act NOW;

otherwise it will be evil rather that goodness that finally prospers. Thirdly, the psalmists' humble acknowledgement before God of what is in their hearts seems to have acted as a safety-valve, ensuring that anger would not turn outwards into violent action or inwards into corrosive bitterness. If at times they seem to be telling God what to do, they are aware of his claim that 'Vengeance is mine' (*Deuteronomy 32:35*) and that he has his own way of defeating enemies – like transforming them into friends. Finally, we can interpret these harsh psalms into an appeal for the destruction of all the evils that afflict us – including our own sinfulness. Better still, we can see them as a challenge, daring us to put into practice the wonderful Christian ideal of loving enemies and doing good to those who ill-treat us[11].

3. Psalms of Instruction

There are some psalms which hardly fall into either of the families we have discussed so far. And so there is need for an additional 'catch-all' category. The psalms of this family might be called 'instructional' because their principal purpose is to teach, to instruct: they teach about the Law, or about the conditions required of those who wish to join in the Temple liturgy, or about Israel's history and its lessons, or about the Wisdom that helps us to face life's fundamental issues, such as the problem of evil or the way to happiness. It may well be these psalms which the GI has specially in mind when it says that 'sometimes difficulties arise ... when the psalm is not addressed directly to God. The psalmist is a poet and often addresses the people as he recalls Israel's history; ... He even represents the words as being spoken by God himself and individual people.. It is in keeping with the poetic and musical character of the psalms that they do not necessarily address God but are sung in his presence' (*GI§105; emphasis added*).

What emerges even from this brief consideration of psalm categories is that the one hundred and fifty psalms that make up the psalter are a rich and variegated anthology. And yet the Hebrews called the whole collection quite simply *Tehillim*, which means 'Praises'. So far as they were concerned, and we'd do well to learn from them, all the psalms, whether they praise or plead or instruct, whether they express gladness or sadness, are at root nothing less than 'poems of praise' to our great God.

The Psalms as Christian Prayers

We have seen that the first step in using the psalms as prayers is to understand what they meant to those by whom and for whom they were written: 'each psalm has its own meaning, which we cannot (afford) to overlook' (*GI§105*). Most of this chapter has been an attempt to help us take that step. Of course we cannot expect these ancient songs to reflect the fullness of revelation that has come to us through Jesus Christ: we will look to them in vain for mention of the Sacraments, for instance, or the Trinity, or Our Lady. Yet even at this first level, i.e. that of taking them in their original sense, many of the psalms serve as ready-made prayers for the believer: they express longing for God, need for his help and mercy, trust and confidence in his unfailing concern, gratitude for his love and faithfulness, and so on. For instance, Psalm 50, 'Have mercy on me, God, in your kindness', has long established itself among Christians as a prayer of repentance, just as it stands. Again, a Christian would have no difficulty in prayerfully reflecting on such sentiments as these:

'The Lord is just in all his ways
and loving in all his deeds.
He is close to all who call on him,
who call on him from their hearts'.
(*Psalm 144; see Evening Prayer, Friday, Week Four*)

Other psalms may not so easily lend themselves to Christian prayer, and yet in fact the whole psalter has, almost since the beginning, been a staple of Christian spirituality and worship. After all, Jesus himself had announced that: 'everything written about me in the law ..., the prophets and the psalms must be fulfilled' (*Luke 24:44; underlining added*). He added that law, prophets and psalms bear witness that 'the Messiah is to suffer and to rise from the dead on the third day, and that repentance and forgiveness of sins is to be proclaimed in his name to all nations' (*ibid 46-47*). His words indicate that there can be a second level of meaning in the psalms, one over and above the one intended by the psalmist; 'those who pray the psalms in the name of the Church,' says GI§109 'should be aware of their full sense'. It is because the psalms are inspired, have God as their ultimate author, that they can carry a weight of meaning ('a full sense') that even the psalmist could not have suspected and which has become clear only in the light of the life and teaching of Jesus. Take, for instance, these words:

'Surely goodness and kindness shall follow me
all the days of my life.
In the Lord's own house shall I dwell
for ever and ever' (*Psalm 23:6*).

Given the Hebrew view of after-life (see p72), what the psalmist had in mind was, almost certainly, a long life on this earth and by 'the Lord's own house' he meant not heaven but the Temple in Jerusalem. However, with the benefit of Christian revelation, we can easily enlarge the meaning of the psalmist's words, 'full-fill' them, by reading them as a promise of eternal life. The psalms may be pre-Christian in origin, but they have acquired a richer meaning since the coming of Jesus Christ. This is particularly so of the 'royal' psalms, which are not to be confused with The 'enthronement psalms (p86), the psalms of God's Kingship. The latter, as we have seen, belong to the category of psalms of praise. However, the 'royal' psalms can belong to any of the three categories we have mentioned (praise, petition or instruction), but – this is the all-important factor – they were written with the human king of the day in mind; they pleaded for his protection in battle, or gave thanks for his victory, or celebrated his coronation and so on. So, for example, Psalm 71 begins: 'O God, give your judgement to the king, to a king's son your justice.' One of the most extraordinary things in Israel's history is the fact that even after the fall of Jerusalem, when the monarchy disappeared for ever, the people continued to use the 'royal' psalms. This was possible only because they had re-interpreted them: they read them and prayed them in a new sense. Since a king was an 'anointed' one (literally, a 'Messiah'), they read these psalms as referring to the future Messiah, the warrior king who they believed would one day deliver them from their enemies and establish God's kingdom.

Christians took reinterpretation a stage further. They quickly realised that the 'Messianic' psalms revealed their fullest and most splendid meaning when they were applied to Jesus Christ, the Messiah who had already come. The language of these psalms which might seem excessive in relation to an ordinary mortal, even a king, is entirely appropriate when applied to Jesus: he is in all truth God's Son, his kingdom will indeed spread to the ends of the earth and last for ever. In fact the opening line of the Messianic Psalm 109 – 'The Lord's (God's) revelation to my Master (the Messiah)' – appears in the New Testament more frequently than any other quotation from the Old Testament. The psalms were regarded as prophetic; thus, Peter boldy preaches about the death and resurrection of Christ in the words of Psalm 118: 'The stone which the builders rejected has become the cornerstone.' Similarly, Psalm 21 ('My God, my God, why have you forsaken me?') and Psalm 68 ('Save me, O God, the waters have risen to my neck') coloured the way in which the evangelists described the passion of Christ; in fact, before the writing of the Gospels, these psalms were 'the principal biblical description of Jesus' passion and death, and occupied a place in the Church's worship similar to that which the (gospel) passion narrative has for us today'[12]. There is no doubt that recognition of the Messianic sense of some of the psalms 'was the reason for the Church's introduction of the (whole) psalter into its prayer' (*GI§109*).

It is instructive to note how often Messianic psalms appear in the Office of Sunday, the day when we celebrate the Easter victory of our Messiah king. And as we follow the Prayer of the Church on a regular basis, we shall become familiar with the way in which the Church 'accommodates' psalms to various events in the life of our Saviour, from his birth in Bethlehem to his Ascension in glory. Much as we can be helped by understanding the psalms at the two levels of which I've spoken – the literal level and the fuller level – understanding is not the same as praying. Thomas Merton suggested that men and women 'of prayer' can be divided into three groups, according to the attitudes they adopt towards the psalms. First are those who theoretically accept that they are a very fine form of prayer, but do little about it. The second are those who have strong convictions about the value of the psalms, but never really enter into them: they recite them with meticulous care but in a rather mechanical fashion. And the third group 'consists of those who know by experience that the psalms are a perfect prayer, a prayer in which Christ prays in the Christian soul, uniting that soul to the Father... They have entered into the psalms with faith. They have in a sense "lived" out the meaning of some of the psalms in their own lives. They have tasted and seen that the Lord is sweet'[13].

Entering into the psalms with faith, living out their meaning. I think of that Indonesian woman who prayed Psalm 142 in prison (see p30 above). How could anyone doubt that she had lived on the inside, so to say, of 'her' psalm? Or I think of a dear friend of mine, a doctor, who died of cancer while still in his early 50s; towards the end, when reduced to little more than a skeleton, he kept just one book under his pillow, the book of psalms. 'These psalms,' he explained, 'are the prayers that mean most to me now.' Or again, I think of a man telling me how the psalms had 'grown more and more luminous with the passing of the years'; but how it had all begun during the dark days of 1940 when, with the drone of aeroplanes overhead and the thud of bombs and clatter of anti-aircraft guns around, his father would gather his family together and pray with them Psalm 90:

He will conceal you with his pinions
and under his wings you will find refuge.
You will not fear the terror of the night,
nor the arrow that flies by day.

'The words of that psalm,' said my correspondent, 'were a lifeline to us.'

Long ago Martin Luther argued that you cannot truly pray a psalm until you have made it your own; until then you are like an actor and, he added with unexpected humour, a shipwrecked person sounds very different from an actor playing the part, even though both use the same words! The psalms do not become our own until they become alive for us, until we begin to live them and pray them in the light of our own experience. In the measure that we have entered the psalms and made them our own, we shall appreciate the Prayer of the Church, and that appreciation will be enhanced still further as we come to recognise – the theme of our next chapter – how intimately the Prayer is linked with the Church's Liturgical Year.

References

1. T Merton *The Psalms are our Prayers* Burns and Oates, London (1957) p6

2. J Magonet – *A Rabbi Reads the Psalms* SCM Press Ltd (1994) p7

3. T Merton *op.cit.* p16

4. David won Jerusalem by scaling the narrow spur to the south east and capturing its citadel, which was known as the mount of Sion and considered to be impregnable; he made it into his own royal city. Only from the days of king Solomon did the city spread northwards and westwards. Jerusalem and Sion both refer to the whole city but Sion is the one which appears most frequently in Israel's poetic writings, such as the psalms.

5. W Brueggemann *The Psalms and the Life of Faith* (collection of Brueggemann's journal articles by P Miller) Fortress Press, Minneapolis (1995) p61

6. W Brueggemann *The Message of the Psalms: A Theological Commentary* – Augsburg Publishing House (1984) – p169

7. Here especially it is important to realise that the 500-year 'volumes' are only approximate. In fact, the Exile and the return from Exile both occured in the 6th century BC. However, to preserve the schematic form we are following, it seems justifiable to number them in volume four.

8. C S Lewis *Reflections on the Psalms* Fontana Books (1973) p12

9. T Craven *The Book of Psalms* The Liturgical Press, Collegeville, Minnesota, (1992) p40

10. The author has published another book, *New Light,* (Redemptorist Publications, 1993), which does offer a brief consideration of each psalm (and canticle) in the order in which it appears in the Prayer of the Church, as well as suggesting the family to which each belongs.

11. Brueggemann writes; 'My hunch is that there is a way *beyond* the psalms of vengeance, but it is a way *through* them and not *around* them.'

12. H Hendrix *The Passion Narratives of the Gospels* Geoffrey Chapman, London (1984) p92

13. T Merton *op.cit.* p18f

5 – Seasons And Saints In The Prayer Of The Church

'How many things by seasons season'd are
To their praise and true perfection.'
(The Merchant of Venice: 5,1)

'Throughout the year the entire mystery of Christ is unfolded and the birthdays (days of death) of the saints are commemorated.'
(General Norms for the Liturgical Year and the Calendar §1)

Chapter two listed five reasons why the Prayer of the Church has an altogether special place in the life of the Church, but also hinted that the list was not complete. Now I want to extend it.

What is so special about this particular prayer? The fact that it is intimately linked with the Church's Liturgical Year and, furthermore, keeps alive the memory of our brothers and sisters, the Saints, and enables us to live out our communion with them. (As we pursue this theme, further light will be thrown on what was said in chapter two about the significance of the Prayer of the Church as liturgical prayer.)

§1. The Liturgical Year

The Paschal Mystery

We have already seen that CL has the distinction of being the first document to be promulgated by the Second Vatican Council. 'It is no exaggeration,' wrote one Protestant commentator, 'to say that (the Constitution on the Liturgy) is ... one of the finest achievements in the long history of Church councils'[1]. Nor, for my part, do I believe it is an exaggeration to add that one of the key results of the Constitution has been the 'recovery' of Easter 'as the oldest and the greatest of the Christian feasts'[2] and, together with that, the recognition that at the heart of the Church and of the whole of the Church's liturgy is the 'Paschal Mystery'[3]. The Paschal Mystery – the phrase owes its popularity in large measure to the writings of a German Benedictine monk, Odo Casel, who in his monastery of Maria Laach devoted his life to the study of the liturgy, and died, with providential appropriateness, just after singing the greeting 'Lumen Christi' (Light of Christ) at the start of the Easter Celebrations in 1948. But what exactly does that phrase mean? The two words of which it is composed – 'paschal' and 'mystery' – are rich in significance and each deserves to be considered on its own.

First, the term 'paschal': it comes from the Greek word pascha, itself a translation of the Hebrew word pesach which means 'passover'. It takes us back to the most decisive event in Jewish history, when God rescued the Israelites from slavery, 'passing over' them when death struck the homes of the Egyptians, and enabling them to 'pass over' to the Promised Land. Thus redeemed by God, they were drawn into a special relationship with him, they became his chosen, covenanted people. And year by year at the feast of the Pasch, they joyfully celebrated what God had done for them; indeed, in 'remembering' those events, they believed that they themselves were in some extraordinary way caught up in them. And yet the mighty deeds of the Exodus were but a foreshadowing of *the* decisive intervention of God which took place in the person of Jesus Christ our Lord. It was not by chance that the climactic events of his life occurred at the time of year when the feast of passover was kept, for it is through those events that all the promises connected with the Jewish passover have been realised: through his death and resurrection we are redeemed, enabled to pass over from the darkness of sin to the light of God's grace, pass over from being sinners to being his beloved children, pass over from death to eternal life. And so St Paul can speak of Christ as the true Pasch, the culmination of all that has gone before. Henceforth, the (new) paschal event – the death and resurrection of Jesus – has become the climax of the history of salvation.

The word that accompanies 'Paschal' is 'Mystery'. In general it suggests something that baffles us, something that is beyond our comprehension. But in theology it has three special levels of meaning: in the first place it refers to

God himself (the 'God-mystery', as we might call it) and in particular to his plan of salvation for the world. Of its nature it is not accessible to our limited human minds and yet it has been revealed to us in love through Jesus Christ; that is why he was able to tell his friends: 'When you have seen me, you have seen the Father' (*John 14:9*).

And so, in the second place, we can speak of the 'Christ-mystery', for he is 'the revelation of God's mystery and in and through him it is finally and fully made manifest'[4]. (Though the God-mystery has been revealed in Christ, it still remains a mystery in the sense that its depths of meaning far exceed the grasp of human understanding.) Jesus manifested God's saving plan by actually bringing it to fulfilment, so that Vatican II can say that 'Christ the Lord completed (his task) principally in the paschal mystery of his blessed passion, resurrection from the dead, and glorious ascension, whereby "dying he destroyed our death and rising, restored our life" ' (*CL§5*). However, if we are to benefit from Jesus' saving work, his paschal mystery, we must in some way be able to share in his death and resurrection – in his mystery, in fact. But how? The answer is: through the liturgy; and so just as we speak of the God-mystery and the Christ-mystery, so also, in the third place, can we speak of the 'liturgy-mystery'. 'The liturgy is the mystery of Christ made present to us ... a symbolic representation of the saving work of Christ in which the reality of that work becomes present ... in so far as it is reproduced in us by the present action of the risen Christ ... and by the active influence of the acts that made up his redemptive work'[5]. And so the meaning of the paschal mystery might finally be summed up as the Christian community sharing in Christ's redeeming death and resurrection by means of worship.

Sunday and the Week

Since, as has been pointed out (see p34f), the Prayer of the Church is one of the principal parts (together with the Eucharist and the sacraments) of the Church's liturgy, it too is not simply a 'recalling' of past redeeming events but a 'recalling' of them (they are called back today for our sakes), in some sense a 'capturing' of them so that the saving Christ-mystery, in all its fullness, is actually made present and available to us. 'Each day is made holy,' says the General Instruction for the Liturgical Year and Calendar, 'through liturgical celebrations of the people of God, especially through the Eucharistic sacrifice and the divine office'[6] (*emphasis added*). This will become clearer as we look at the pattern of the liturgical year.

One of the most striking features of Christianity is that it takes time seriously. It does so because 'it is through actual events happening in historical time that ... God is revealed'. For example, Luke's gospel opens with the words: 'In the days of King Herod of Judea ...' (*Luke 1:5*): the events that are about to be described took place in time, not in the 'once upon a time' of fairy stories but in the real time which we ourselves occupy, the time which is measured by the clock and the calendar, the time in which people work and raise families, and wash the car and go to work and do the shopping. The 'centrality of time in Christianity is reflected in Christian worship'[7], for its essential structure is based upon recurring rhythms of the day, the week, the year, the season.

At one time Sunday was the one and only feast day celebrated by the Church, and so it is rightly described as 'the original feast day' and 'the foundation and kernel of the entire liturgical year' (*CL§106*). Every Sunday is a 'little Easter', the day of the week when the whole paschal mystery is celebrated. From the start it was known as 'the Lord's day', the day of Christ, because it is the day of his resurrection. However, because the resurrection occurred on 'the first day of the week', it is also referred to as the 'first day'[8], the day above all others when the local church meets in its eucharistic assembly. One of the main aims – and achievements – of Vatican II was to restore the significance of Sunday: 'because of (its) unique dignity ... other celebrations are not to take its place unless they are of truly great importance'[9]. Each of the thirty-odd Sundays of Ordinary Time (see below) is a celebration of Easter, each is a feast, and its paschal character is to be seen not only in the Mass but also in the Prayer of the Church. This is why GI§207 says that on Sunday 'it is of great advantage to celebrate ... at least evening prayer, in keeping with a very ancient tradition'. Every Sunday the Liturgy of the Hours includes the singing of psalms that are evocative of the paschal mystery: Psalm 117 ('Give thanks to the Lord, for he is good'), which is sung at Morning Prayer on the second and fourth Sundays and at Daytime Prayer on the first and third Sundays, is the song of thanksgiving of a victorious king and includes phrases eminently appropriate to the day of resurrection ('This day was made by the Lord; we rejoice and are glad') and to our Risen Lord himself ('the stone which the builders rejected has become the corner stone; this is the work of the Lord, a marvel in our eyes'). The canticle at Morning Prayer on Sunday is either Daniel 3:57-88 ('O all you works of the Lord, O bless the Lord') which summons the whole of creation to praise the Lord, or Daniel 3:52-57 ('You are blest, Lord God of our fathers') which acknowledges that universal praise is already rendered to him: it was through Christ, the Word of God, that all things came into being; it is through the Risen Christ that all have been re-created. Finally, at Evening Prayer II the first psalm is always 109 ('The Lord's revelation to my Master'), which sings of the Messiah who in his dying and rising has been revealed as King and Priest.

Easter and the Year

Just as Sunday is at the heart of the weekly cycle, so Easter itself is at the heart of the annual cycle and from it there fans out the whole liturgical year (or Church year) which was built up gradually over succeeding generations. Towards the end of the fourth century, a Spanish lady named Egeria, possibly a nun, went on pilgrimage to the Holy Land and has left us a fascinating picture of the celebrations that took place there at Easter time. On the first day of 'The Great Week' (i.e. Palm Sunday) there was a procession in which the worshippers bore palms and which descended the Mount of Olives and entered the city of Jerusalem. On the next three days there were minor ceremonies, though on Wednesday ('Spy Wednesday') the story of Judas' betrayal was always read; on Thursday everyone received Holy Communion and the bishop and congregation then went to the Garden of Gethsemane; on Friday ('Good Friday') a service was held on mount Calvary, with veneration of a relic of the true Cross and Holy Communion received from the reserved Sacrament. Saturday was a day of fasting and the celebration of Easter began with a lengthy vigil and culminated in the joyous celebration of the Eucharist after midnight.

It is not difficult to discern in this account the skeleton of our current Holy Week, crowned as it is with the 'Sacred Triduum' (the sacred three days) which begins at sunset on Maundy Thursday and continues until sunset on Easter Day. As the diagram below indicates, this core festival was preceded and followed by two 'seasons'.

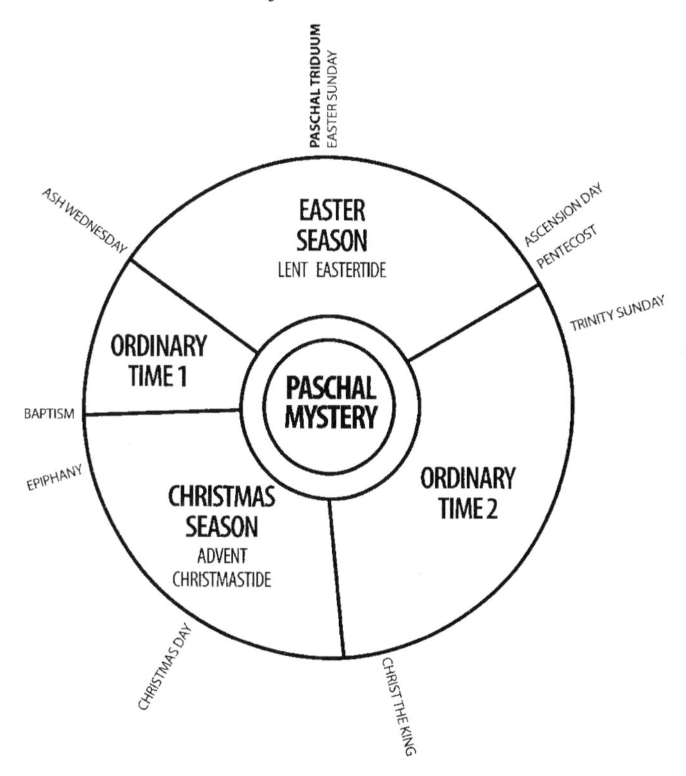

The first is the Lenten season, the forty days of preparation for the great feast[10]; the second, far older and more important than Lent, is the Easter season, 'the Great Fifty Days', which are viewed as a single whole, even as a single day, one great Sunday, stretching from Easter Sunday to the feast of Pentecost, which brings 'the paschal mystery to its completion'[11] for Jesus sent us the Holy Spirit, from the Father, 'to complete his work on earth and bring us the fullness of grace'[12]. (It includes the feast of the Ascension, though that too is an aspect of the resurrection.) There is no doubting the centrality of Easter in the life and liturgy of the Church once we realise that the resurrection is commemorated not only by a day each week (Sunday) and a feast each year (Easter Day) but also by a complete season (Eastertide). 'The risen Christ is the star which illuminates our whole year'[13].

Our 'Year of Grace'

'In the course of the year, (the Church) unfolds the whole mystery of Christ from the incarnation and nativity to the ascension, to Pentecost and the expectation of the ... coming of the Lord. Thus recalling the mysteries of the redemption, it opens up to the faithful the riches of the Lord's power and merits, so that these are in some way made present at all times; the faithful lay hold of them and are filled with saving grace' (*CL§102*).

Pius Parsch, the author of a celebrated five-volumed work on the liturgical cycle[14], speaks of that cycle as 'the Church's year of grace'. It would be hard to find a simpler or more admirable description. Through its feasts and seasons, week by week, and year by year, the Church is constantly reminding us of the saving work of Jesus Christ, unfolding again and again the story of our salvation; but that is not all, for as we recall these past events and give thanks for them, their saving power is offered to us anew. The liturgical year, therefore, encompasses past, present and future: past, in that it commemorates what has been accomplished for us by our Saviour; the present in that it draws us here and now into the beneficial effects of the Lord's saving activity; and the future in that it prepares us for, and even gives us a foretaste of, the heavenly banquet at the end of history.

The cycle begins with Advent, when we joyfully re-live the ancient expectation of the birth of Christ, the Messiah, but also prepare for his second coming in glory at the end of time. Advent reaches its climax on Christmas Day, when we celebrate the lowly birth of God's son: 'the Word (through whom all things were made and by whom all remain in existence) was made flesh and dwelt amongst us'; he joined the human race, became one of us. Far from being independent of Easter, even the Christmas festival 'links us to the beginnings of the paschal mystery ... (it) prepares us to understand Easter better by showing the Redeemer to be the very Son of God made man'[15]. The celebration of Christ's birth, like that of his resurrection, continues for eight days (an octave). The import of his nativity is underlined by the feast of the Epiphany (from a Greek word meaning 'manifestation'), whose liturgy makes it clear that this is a feast with several layers of meaning. 'Today,' says the Magnificat antiphon, 'the star led the Magi to the manger; today water was changed into wine at the marriage feast; today Christ desired to be baptised by John in the river Jordan to bring salvation.' Thus, in addition to the manifestation of Jesus to the Gentiles, in the persons of the wise men from afar, there is also the manifestation brought about by the miracle at Cana when 'he let his glory be seen' and the manifestation of his baptism when a voice from heaven proclaimed him to be the Son of God. The Christmas season is finally brought to a close by the feast of the Baptism. In the waters of the Jordan Jesus was manifested as the Son of God and at the same time began the public mission which would lead him finally to the cross and beyond that to Easter.

Lent, beginning on Ash Wednesday, is the next distinctive season. It is characterised by two related themes – the first, baptism (either recalled or prepared for) and the other, penitence – which are intended to renew the community in preparation for the celebration of the Paschal Mystery. As we have seen, the period in Holy Week from Thursday evening until Sunday morning forms one whole, the Paschal Triduum, with the Vigil as its crown, and it is followed by the season of Eastertide (or Paschaltide) which continues for the next seven weeks until the feast of Pentecost.

What remains of the liturgical year, the part which falls outside the great seasons just described, is called 'Ordinary time', though that must not be taken to mean that it is of little importance, that it is in no way special. On the contrary, it is only in the manner of its unfolding the mystery of Christ that Ordinary time differs from any other, for instead of one or other aspect of Christ's mystery being singled out, it is 'the mystery of Christ in all its fullness (which) is celebrated'[16] each week in Ordinary time. It is made up of thirty-three or thirty-four Sundays, the last being the solemnity of Christ the King. Because Easter is a moveable feast, there is a slight variation in the number and disposition of the Sundays of Ordinary time from one year to another: up to eight Ordinary Sundays occur between the feast of the Baptism and the beginning of Lent, and the rest fall between the Easter and Christmas cycles. In the latter part of the Ordinary cycle there are three major festivals (or solemnities) of the Lord – the Most Holy Trinity, the Body and Blood of Christ and the Most Sacred Heart of Jesus – the first of them falling on the Sunday after Pentecost. In general, the Sundays in Ordinary time centre upon Jesus' public life, teaching and ministry, though the final weeks focus more especially on his second coming, and so lead naturally into the season of Advent once again, and, with it, the beginning of another 'year of grace'.

There are two vital points that must be made at the end of this section. The first is that in speaking of a 'cycle' in the Church's year, and even suggesting that the cycle 'begins again', it may sound as though we are like small children who, having heard the oft-repeated bed-time story, are always ready to cry out 'Again!' – and woe betide any narrator who goes astray in the telling of the story! But strictly speaking the liturgical year is not 'the same old story' repeated times without number; indeed – despite the diagram on page 100 above – it should be represented not so much by a circle as by a spiral staircase. The latter may cover the same ground over and over again, but never at exactly the same level: it ascends ever higher and it descends ever deeper. Though in the liturgy the same sacred events are celebrated each year, yet in a very real sense no two annual celebrations are the same. Just as each anniversary of a wedding or of ordination is unique, drawing the person(s) involved into a growing appreciation of married life or priestly life, so each year's liturgical celebrations enable the Church – and we are the Church – to penetrate more deeply, become involved at a still deeper level in the saving mysteries of Christ. 'Great are the works of the Lord,' cries the psalmist, 'to be pondered by all who love them' (*Psalm 110:2*). It is supremely through the liturgy that we are given the opportunity for that prayerful pondering, at ever greater depths, of the 'great works of the

Lord'. In this connection the famous lines of T S Eliot's Little Gidding are particularly apposite:

We shall not cease from exploration
And the end of all our exploring
Will be to arrive where we started
And know the place for the first time[17].

Each time the Church's year spins round, '(the Lord) makes us remember his wonders' (*Psalm 110*) with all the freshness of a 'first time' encounter.

But even that is not quite all: corresponding to the descent (the ever deeper) there is also an ascent (the ever higher and ever further): the liturgical cycle is not a closed circle hemming us in but a spiral, drawing us to different levels; year by year, in the company of all God's pilgrim people, it is leading us onwards and upwards, ever closer to the end–time when this world's history is completed and its liturgy is no more, for the saving work of Christ will have finally been consummated.

The second point that must be made is that while the Eucharist is the summit of liturgical activity, yet, as we have had occasion to mention more than once, the Prayer of the Church is an integral part of the liturgy: it too faithfully reflects all the seasons and festivals of the year. It is not possible in a book of this size to explain in detail all the variations that occur in the Prayer of the Church at different times in scriptural readings, hymns, antiphons, intercessions, prayers, etc – not all are to be found in the simplified editions of The Divine Office – though something more will be said about them later in the chapter. However as you pray the Office, following the directions given in the breviary, you will discover for yourself the special items that indicate a particular season or a particular festival; and when that happens you will also have the joy of discovering that the Prayer of the Church is a powerful way of keying into the liturgical year. Together with the Mass, and in dependence upon the Mass, it invites us to meditate prayerfully on all the events that make up the Christ-mystery from his birth in Bethlehem to his return in glory at the end of time. But, like the Mass, the Prayer of the Church goes much further than merely recalling past events or even giving us the opportunity to meditate upon them. Odo Casel used to say that Christ has to become in a sense our contemporary; and that is precisely what is made possible through the liturgy, including the Prayer of the Church: the mysteries of our redemption are made present to us in our day in such a way that we are able to lay hold of them and so be filled with grace.

§2. Celebrating the Saints

'It is especially in the sacred liturgy that our union with the heavenly church is best realised' (Vatican II's Constitution on the Church §50).

We live in an age of technological progress, from the jet engine to the internet, which has in astonishing fashion concertinaed distances and brought people closer to each other, but the liturgy spans a barrier which no technology could ever cross, that dividing this world from the next. Not only does it bring us into closest union with our Saviour Jesus Christ but also with all those 'who have left this world in (God's) friendship'; it sharpens our awareness of the communion of saints[18] and enables us to make it a reality. In the letter to the Hebrews, we are reminded that Jesus himself is 'the pioneer of faith', our chief example and model. Nothing must come between us and him, but that same letter also reminds us that we are part of a great company and that the dazzling holiness of the Lord is broken down, so to say, in a way that we can perhaps more easily appreciate it in the lives of men and women who 'have been made perfect'. We are pictured, in the letter to the Hebrews, as athletes in a race, and there is no shortage of spectators: the saints are like 'a great cloud of witnesses all around' us, urging us on to 'run through patience the race that lies before us' (*12:1*). However, the saints are not like those tiresome parents at a sports day who urge their youngsters to do what they could never have achieved themselves! They make a contribution to our 'race' by offering us their example to inspire us, their prayers to support us and, more even than that, their victory as something in which we already have a share – albeit not yet in its fullness. Because we are one Body in Christ, members one of another, what affects one, affects all; the final victory is ours – even if 'not yet'.

Without in any way denying what has just been said, it has to be admitted that there was a time not so long ago when the saints occupied a disproportionate place in the liturgy: not only did saints' days occur on almost every day of the year, but also, and much more seriously, they threatened to divert attention from the mysteries of Christ. Accordingly, in the aftermath of Vatican II two things have happened in the liturgy, and therefore in the Prayer of the Church: saints' days have been reduced in number and in general their celebrations have been re-evaluated, so that the celebration of Sunday can never be replaced except by feasts of the Lord himself[19] or by those festivals known as solemnities (see below). Moreover, the calendar of saints is presented as clearly subsidiary to, and to some degree dependent upon, the liturgical year. And so the Church makes 'proper provision for the rightful honouring of individual saints ... in the liturgy of the hours' but at the same time ensures that 'the celebrations of the saints are arranged so that that they do not take precedence over those feast days and special seasons that commemorate the mysteries of salvation' (*GI§218*). The significance of these changes will become clearer in the following sections which deal with the place of Mary and the Saints in the liturgy.

Blessed Mary, Mother of God

Among the saints, Mary is without compare; she holds – and has held since early times – a unique place in the life and liturgy of the Church. 'In celebrating (the) annual cycle of the mysteries of Christ,' says CL§103, 'the Church honours the blessed Mary, Mother of God, with special love.' (The honouring of Mary is expressly linked with 'the annual cycle of the mysteries of Christ'.) By way of explanation the document notes first that Mary 'is inseparably linked with her Son's saving work', second that she is 'the most excellent fruit' of that work and, third, that she is 'a faultless image' of the final state of perfection which the Church desires for all its members. The honouring of Mary, therefore, is a truly Christian devotion because, in the words of Paul VI, 'it takes its origin and effectiveness from Christ, finds its complete expression in Christ, and leads through Christ in the Spirit to the Father'[20].

That Mary's place in the liturgy is closely connected with the annual cycle of the mysteries of her Son becomes clear as we glance at her feasts throughout the year. In Advent, besides other references to her in the Prayer of the Church, there is the celebration of her Immaculate Conception on December 8, a feast which not only honours Mary but also celebrates the beginning of preparations for the coming of the Saviour, as well as the beginning of the Church 'without spot or wrinkle'. The Christmas season itself might be described as a prolonged commemoration of Mary's divine Motherhood: in adoring the Son, we also venerate the Mother. On January 1 stands the solemnity of 'Mary the Holy Mother of God' and on February 2 the 'Presentation of the Lord', a festival which commemorates both Mother and Son. Closely allied to the Christmas season is the feast of the Annunciation (March 25), which again honours both Christ and the Blessed Virgin. And finally comes the feast of the Assumption (August 15), the culmination of the Marian feasts, and the celebration of the crowning fruit of the redeeming work of her Son. Throughout the year there are other lesser celebrations of saving events in which Mary is associated with Jesus: her Birthday (September 8), the Visitation (May 31), the commemoration of Our Lady of Sorrows (September 15); and in addition there are celebrations of local devotions which have gained wide popularity, such as that of Our Lady of Lourdes (February 11) and Our Lady of the Rosary (October 7). In showing how 'the Liturgy of the Hours ... contains outstanding examples of devotion to the Mother of the Lord', Paul VI makes special reference to some of the hymns, antiphons and intercessions at Morning and Evening Prayer; he might also have added that on the majority of Saturdays in Ordinary Time throughout the year a Memorial of the Blessed Virgin may be celebrated. Moreover, Mary's prayer par excellence, the Magnificat, always has a place at Evening Prayer and it is with one of her anthems, such as the 'Hail, Holy Queen' that Night Prayer ends and the whole Prayer of the Church for that day reaches its conclusion.

The Saints

The supreme significance of the saints, according to CL§111, is that 'they proclaim the wonderful works of Christ in his servants' and 'offer to the faithful fitting examples for their imitation'. Furthermore, by celebrating 'the day they died' (i.e. their birthday into heaven) the Church 'proclaims the paschal mystery in the saints who have suffered and have been glorified with Christ'. Once again, the unique importance of Christ and his paschal mystery are underlined. The Church rightly sets the saints before us, because to be familiar with them is a way of discovering Christ more fully, for it is on him that they modelled their lives, in him they found their inspiration, from him they received the grace of exceptional holiness. That is why there is a long tradition, stretching back to at least the second century, of devotion to the saints, beginning with the martyrs and finally embracing men and women of all lands and all conditions of life who have given proof of outstanding sanctity.

This long tradition must of course continue, but, as CL insisted, 'the feasts of the saints (must not) take precedence over the feasts which commemorate the actual mysteries of salvation' and 'only those (saints' days) should be extended to the universal Church which commemorate saints of truly universal importance' (*§111*). The 'General Calendar', which was drawn up after the Council, includes saints who have such a universal significance (St Joseph and St John the Baptist, for example, both closely connected with the Saviour's work) or saints who are judged to have a particular appeal for the contemporary Church and demonstrate the abiding presence of holiness among the people of God (St Francis of Assisi or St Thérèse of Lisieux would be good examples). In addition to the General Calendar, there are also 'National Calendars' which enable a diocese or a national church to honour in a special way saints who are specially associated with it. Thus, in England the feast of the English Martyrs and the feast of St George are celebrated, and in the different dioceses of the country particular diocesan patrons are similarly honoured. (Neither the General nor the National Calendar of saints features in the simplified breviary, 'A Shorter Morning and Evening Prayer'.)

Celebrating Saints' Days

In the breviary, the saints are dealt with under two general headings. The first, 'The Proper of Saints', offers a very brief biography of each saint under the date that he or she appears in the Calendar; it also provides those parts of the Office that are 'proper', in the sense that they are particular to this or that saint. The second, 'The Common Offices', gives a series of Offices (readings, antiphons, etc) for various categories of saints; so there is the Common of Martyrs, the Common of Pastors, the Common of Virgins, and so on.

Saints' days are all ranked, in order of importance, as either 'solemnities', 'feasts' or 'memorials'. Only the most outstanding celebrations, such as that of All Saints, November 1, or the great festivals of our Lady, fall into the category of *solemnities*; in fact in the General Calendar there are less than twenty of them. On these days, just as on Sundays (see page 59), there are two Evening Prayers, one on the eve of the celebration and the other on the day itself; in addition, many parts of the Office are 'proper', they belong exclusively to this or that saint's day. Celebrations of the second rank, the *feasts*, are more numerous and they, too, almost always contain some elements which are proper; so, for example, on the feast of St Thérèse, October 1, there is a special antiphon before the Benedictus at Morning Prayer which is particularly appropriate for a saint renowned for her 'little way': it is our Lord's words:

"Indeed I tell you that, unless you undergo a change of heart and become more like children, you shall not enter my heavenly kingdom."

Most numerous of all are the celebrations classified as *memorials*, and – wait for it! – these are further subdivided into two categories: a memorial is either 'obligatory' or 'optional'. That means, broadly speaking, that while the first will normally be celebrated, unless there are strong reasons to the contrary, a decision to celebrate the latter is left entirely to the choice of the leader (though, one would hope, in consultation with the congregation or at least with a sound awareness of its likely wishes in the matter) or, in private celebration, with the individual. Generally, the prayer of a memorial is proper, and sometimes other parts of the Office also, but as a rule the major elements will come from one of the Common Offices, as explained above.

There are other rather technical matters concerned with the honouring of saints in the Prayer of the Church – such as the precise relationship of one celebration to another or under what circumstances a celebration which falls, say, in Lent can be transferred to another time – but these need not bother us, particularly in the early days of praying the Prayer of the Church. Indeed, it may be useful at that stage to omit the celebration of saints' days altogether, and simply follow the Offices for Sundays and the ordinary days of the week. There will be plenty of time later to begin celebrating the saints, and, as has been mentioned, you will find helpful directions in the breviary itself, so that in a short time you will become as adept at coping with a saint's day as with any other.

We must always bear in mind what was said in an earlier chapter, that the most important aspect of the Prayer of the Church is that it is a prayer; anything that diverts us from that is to be avoided. And so the simple rule is to use the Prayer of the Church in the way that is most helpful to us, not thinking of it primarily, let alone simply, in terms of rules and regulations. Let me give a specific example: newcomers sometimes find it disconcerting that the psalms indicated for Morning Prayer in every one of the Common Offices are those of Morning Prayer of Sunday in Week One; but that in turn means that if there are several saints to be celebrated within a few days we could be repeating the same psalms day after day. The psalms of Morning Prayer of Sunday One are particularly beautiful, yet even they can become wearisome if used constantly; it is good, therefore, that we should feel free to use the full range of psalms that are available to us. And so we ought not to hesitate to use the psalms of the appropriate day of the week, rather than those indicated in the Common, if that will help our prayer.

As we come to the end of this chapter it is, I think, worth insisting once again that, whatever else happens, we must not allow ourselves to become so preoccupied with following the niceties of the rubrics that we lose sight of the profound truths with which these pages have been concerned: in the first place, that the Prayer of the Church is one of the privileged ways we have of keeping in step with the Church in its celebration of the great mysteries of our redemption year after year, of drawing close to the paschal mystery which stands at the heart of the liturgy and suffuses the whole of the year with its brightness, and of sharing in the graces of the Saviour; and, in the second place, that in honouring the special friends of the Lord, Mary and the saints, we become more keenly aware of the effects of the paschal mystery which are revealed in their lives. We realise that, as our brothers and sisters, they assist us by their prayers and we are comforted at the thought of the glorious company to which we belong.

And so we are ready for our final chapter, in which we shall be considering those parts of the Prayer of the Church which we have not dealt with explicitly so far. In doing so, we shall learn something more about the way in which the Prayer of the Church sanctifies not only the weeks and months and years of life, but also the whole of every day.

References

1. L Briner – *A Protestant Looks at the New Constitution on the Sacred Liturgy* p7/8 quoted in *The Second Vatican Council* (ed B Pawley) OUP (1967) p149

2. V Ryan *Pasch to Pentecost* Veritas Publications, Dublin (1977) p7

3. However, it must be said that the re–evaluation of Easter began in 1951 with Pius XII's restoration of the Easter Vigil.

4. J Empereur *The New Dictionary of Theology* Gill & Macmillan, Dublin (1990) p745.

5. C Davis *Liturgy and Doctrine* Sheed & Ward, London (1960) p63

6. *The Liturgy Documents* §3 p173

7. P White *Introduction to Christian Worship* Abingdon Press, Nashville (rev. ed.1990) pp52–3

8. Sunday was also known as the 'eighth day': God completed his creation of the world on the Sabbath (the seventh day) but Jesus' death and resurrection usher in the new creation.

9. J Crichton *The Church's Worship: Considerations on the Liturgical Constitution of the Second Vatican Council*, Geoffrey Chapman, London (1964) p203

10. Originally it was also a time of preparation for those under instruction who were due to be received into the Church at the Easter Vigil as well as for penitents who sought reconciliation.

11. From the Preface for Pentecost

12. From Eucharistic Prayer IV

13. J Lebon *How to Understand the Liturgy* SCM Press, London (1987) p88

14. P Parsch *The Church's Year of Grace* The Liturgical Press, Collegeville, Minnesota (1964-5)

15. P Journel *The Church at Prayer* The Liturgical Press, Collegeville, Minnesota (1985) p82

16. *General Norms for the Liturgical Year and the Calendar* (1969) §43

17. T S Eliot 'Little Gidding', the fourth of 'Four Quartets', in *Collected Poems 1909–1962* Faber & Faber Ltd, London (reprinted 1975) – p222

18. The expression 'communion of saints' refers both to the company of the 'holy ones' and the sharing in 'holy things', above all the Eucharist. It is of course in the former sense we are using it here.

19. The Sundays of Advent, Lent and Eastertide take precedence even over solemnities and feasts of the Lord.

20. The Apostolic Exhortation *Marialis Cultus* promulgated in February 1974 – Catholic Truth Society Do462, p9

6 – Praying The Prayer Of The Church (ii) – Prayer During The Day, Night Prayer, Office of Readings

'Each day is made holy through liturgical celebrations of God's people, especially the eucharistic sacrifice and the divine office.' (General Norms for the Liturgical Year and the Calendar §3)

At the beginning of the Easter Vigil, the celebrant takes the Paschal Candle, a symbol of the risen Christ, and traces upon it the first and last letters of the Greek alphabet (alpha and omega) and the numerals of the current year, saying as he does so:

> 'Christ yesterday and today, the beginning and the end, Alpha and Omega, all times belong to him, and all the ages, to him be glory and power through every age for ever.'

The meaning of the ceremony is clear; in the words of Pope John Paul II:

> 'it emphasizes the fact that *Christ is the Lord of time*; he is its beginning and its end; every year, every day and every moment are embraced by his Incarnation and Resurrection ... For this reason, the Church too lives and celebrates the liturgy ... which in a certain way reproduces the whole mystery of the Incarnation and Redemption'[1].

We have already seen that the Prayer of the Church is also called the Liturgy of the Hours because its outstanding feature is that its various parts cover, and thereby sanctify, the whole of the day. So far we have concerned ourselves almost exclusively with its two principal Hours – Morning Prayer and Evening Prayer; to have prayed these two Hours is already to have prayed the heart of the Church's daily Office. However, a growing number of people, especially though not exclusively among those who are retired, have the desire, and many more, such as the clergy, also have the official mandate, to pray the whole of the Office each day. And so our task now is to consider the other Hours that make up the complete Prayer of the Church, namely, Prayer During the Day, Night Prayer and the Office of Readings.

The first thing to notice is that these 'new' Hours follow exactly the same pattern as that of Morning Prayer and Evening Prayer, though individual parts, such as the Scripture Reading or the psalms, may play a greater or lesser role. Thus, we find the following basic structure in each of the Hours:

Introduction
Psalm(s)
Scripture Reading
Concluding Prayer

Prayer During The Day

You will recall from chapter one that very early in the Church's history the practice of praying three times during the day – at 9 o'clock in the morning (Terce), at midday (Sext) and at 3 o'clock in the afternoon (None) – had taken a firm hold among the people of God. Tertullian, a famous Christian lawyer and writer who died early in the third century and has been called 'the father of Western theology', suggests that these three times of prayer were chosen because they are 'the most important hours in scripture', the hours when the first important steps in the spreading of the Good News took place: at the third hour (9 am) on Pentecost day the Holy Spirit came down upon the Apostles (*Acts 2:15)*, at the sixth hour (midday) it was revealed to Peter, while he was at prayer, that Gentiles could become Christians without observing the Jewish regulations (*Acts 10,9ff*), and at the ninth hour (3 pm) the paralytic was cured by Peter and John as they entered the Beautiful Gate of the Temple for prayer (*Acts 3:1-2*). Later, as we have seen, Christians began to superimpose upon this explanation from the Acts of the Apostles another explanation deriving from the times of the various stages in the passion of the Lord.

Throughout the following centuries these three Hours of prayer, sometimes called the 'little hours' to distinguish them from the 'major hours' of Morning Prayer and Evening Prayer, continued to be observed in the Church. When at Vatican II the Divine Office came under careful scrutiny, it was decided that all three Hours (now re-named 'Prayer before Noon', 'Midday Prayer' and 'Afternoon Prayer') should be retained, though with a significant qualification. The basis for this decision was not only the historical importance of the three Hours but also their spiritual value: by inviting us to pause and reflect for a short time during our work, they are meant to remind us of the ideal of ceaseless prayer and at the same time to keep us mindful 'of the events of the Lord's passion and of the first preaching of the Gospel' (*GI§76*). However, the significant qualification just alluded to is this: whereas in the past those who prayed the complete Office were expected to include all three of the Hours during the day, the GI expressly states that this is no longer the case: 'the liturgical practice of saying these three hours is to be retained ... by those who live the contemplative life' (*underlining added*). It is also recommended for other occasions, such as during 'retreats or pastoral meetings', but, for all practical purposes, those who wish to pray the whole Office are simply expected to 'choose from the three hours the one most appropriate to the time of day' (*GI§76-77*), that is to say, to follow either Prayer before Noon or Midday Prayer or Prayer in the Afternoon. This is a welcome ruling for it enables the busy priest, as well as many a lay person, to maintain 'the tradition of praying in the midst of the day's work' [*GI§77*], without at the same time overburdening themselves with too many interruptions in the course of the day. Those who framed the new breviary have obviously borne in mind what was said at Vatican II: that 'account must be taken of the conditions of modern life especially as they affect those who are engaged in apostolic work' (*CL§89*).

Prayer During the Day has a simple format: it begins in the usual way with a versicle (*O God, come to our aid*) and response (*Lord, make haste to help us*), followed by the

'Glory be to the Father'. Next comes a hymn, which recalls the significance of the Hour and/or the events of salvation, such as the coming of the Holy Spirit, which it brings to mind. Then, there are three psalms (or parts of a psalm) with their accompanying antiphons, and a short Scripture reading (varying according to the time of day – Before Noon, Midday or Afternoon), followed by a versicle by way of response to the word of God. Finally, there is a concluding prayer and, at least in public worship, the acclamation: *Let us bless the Lord* with its response: *Thanks be to God*. (In the special seasons of the year and on feast days, there are special texts for the Readings, antiphons, etc, and these are indicated in the breviary.)

For this Hour of the Prayer of the Church, different psalms are allotted to each day of the four week cycle. In accordance with an ancient Roman tradition, a verse (or section) of Psalm 118 is included in virtually every Prayer During the Day (*see Appendix II*). This psalm, you may remember, is not only the longest in the psalter; it is also an 'alphabetical' psalm, but an alphabetical psalm with a difference. The normal pattern of such a psalm is to take as the first letter in each line, the twenty-two letters of the Hebrew alphabet in sequence; but in Psalm 118 not simply one line but each of the eight lines which make up a verse begins with the same Hebrew letter. The late Monsignor Ronnie Knox tried to capture this feature in his translation of the psalms; for example, his version of the fourth section (the equivalent of our English 'D') runs like this:

Deep lies my soul in the dust, restore life to me as thou hast promised.
Deign now, to shew me thy will, thou who hast listened when I opened my heart to thee.
Direct me in the path thou biddest me follow, and all my musing shall be of thy wonderful deeds.
Despair wrings tears from me; let thy promises raise me up once more.
Deliver me from every false thought; let thy covenant be my comfort.
Duty's path my choice, I keep thy bidding ever in remembrance.
Disappoint me, Lord, never, one that holds fast by thy commandments.
Do but open my heart wide, and easy lies the path thou hast decreed.

Though the translation in the breviary does not emulate Knox in this respect, it does give an indication of the unique character of the psalm by what may seem to newcomers a rather puzzling feature: a heading appears before each section of the psalm that looks like this:

Psalm 118(119):9-16 II (Beth)

As you see, in addition to the customary numbering of the psalm, there is an additional number in Roman numerals (in this case II), followed, in brackets, by the name of one of the letters of the Hebrew alphabet (in this case Beth). Both additions tells us the same thing: that this part of the psalm is section two, the second section, of Psalm 118, i.e. the verse whose eight lines each begin with the Hebrew letter Beth (roughly equivalent to the English 'B').

In addition to the psalms that are arranged for ordinary daily use, there is another collection called the 'complementary psalmody', which appears in the full breviary immediately after Night Prayer. It is intended for the use of those who say all three Hours of Prayer During the Day; they pray the ordinary current psalms at one Hour and then, for the sake of variety, the complementary psalms at the other two. However, when solemnities fall upon a weekday, even those who pray only one of the three Hours are invited to take the psalms from the complementary group. It is worthy of note that the complementary psalms come from a group of psalms commonly referred to as 'the songs of ascent' (psalms 119-134), which seem to have been used by the Jews when they 'went up' (ascended) to Jerusalem on pilgrimage for the celebration of the great feasts. On the whole, these psalms are particularly attractive: Psalm 120 ('I lift up my eyes to the mountains'), for instance, assures us that the Lord, our guardian, who never sleeps or slumbers, takes care of all our comings and goings; Psalm 122 ('To you have I lifted up my eyes') pictures us waiting, like a servant, upon the will of our Master; Psalm 124 ('Those who put their trust in the Lord') reminds us that those who trust in the Lord are as safe as mount Sion, surrounded as it is by protective mountains; Psalm 126 ('If the Lord does not build the house'), which might be described as the prayer of the workaholic, gently admonishes us that our late nights and early mornings will all be in vain unless the Lord is on our side: it is on him, not on us, that the venture ultimately rests.

However, the songs of ascent are not only beautiful in their own right; because of their brevity, they can also easily be memorised. This means that it is possible to recite them by heart even in the midst of work, like the woman I knew who, having learned a few of the psalms, used to pray them while feeding her baby. She was certainly making sure of her Prayer During the Day!

Night Prayer

This Hour concludes the Prayer of the Church each day. It is not to be confused with Evening Prayer, for it is meant to be the last act of the day, to be 'said before retiring' (for the night) explains GI§84, and then, with awareness of modern habits, it adds: 'even if that is after midnight'. And even then, it forms the final part of the Office of the day which is about to be brought to a close.

Like the other Hours, it begins with the appeal: '*O God, come to our aid* ...' and the 'Glory be to the Father'. After this, 'it is a laudable practice to have ... an examination of conscience' (*GI§86*) and an act of sorrow. Where the Hour is celebrated in common, the examination of conscience may take place in silence or may adopt one of the formulas used at the penitential rite at the beginning of Mass; it may prove helpful to look back in silence on the day that has gone, to discern how the Lord has prompted us and how we have responded or failed to do so. Next comes a hymn and then the psalm(s), but, taking cognisance of the fact that we are probably jaded at the end of the day, Night Prayer asks us to pray just one psalm, or, as happens on a couple of occasions, two short psalms; and they are for the most part psalms 'full of confidence in the Lord' (*GI§88*). Because the Office of the Lord's Day begins on the eve of Sunday, i.e. Saturday evening (see page 59), two sets of Night Prayer are provided for Sundays (as well as for Solemnities), the first headed 'After Evening Prayer I of Sundays and Solemnities' and the second 'After Evening Prayer II of Sundays and Solemnities'. Psalm 90 ('He who dwells in the shelter of the Most High'), which features in the second of these Night Prayers for Sunday, has a long tradition behind it as a night prayer: St Basil the Great, the 4th century bishop of Caesarea, seems to have been responsible for the introduction of a time of prayer before going to rest at the end of the day; he writes as follows: 'To ensure a peaceful ... sleep, they shall say Psalm (90) at this moment'[2]. It is a psalm powerful in images of God's unfailing protection at every hour of day and night; he conceals us safely under his wings, he is our refuge and our stronghold, our buckler and shield. The explicit statement that the two Sunday Night Prayers may be used on any night of the week (*GI§88*) is a pleasing touch: it makes it possible for a person to pray Night Prayer by heart (even in bed?) when arriving home late at night. Moreover, those who regularly use one of the Sunday night Offices throughout the week, do not thereby deprive themselves of psalms that would otherwise be used, because the psalms given for Night Prayer on the week nights, from Monday to Friday, also occur elsewhere in the cycle of the Prayer of the Church.

After the psalm(s), there is a scripture reading, followed by a responsory which – very fittingly, as we shall see – includes our Lord's words on the Cross, his final words before death: 'Into your hands, Lord, I commend my spirit.' However, the climax of the Hour is reached with the Canticle of Simeon: 'At last, all powerful Master, you give leave to your servant to go in peace.' These words were spoken by the aged Simeon when Jesus, brought by Mary and Joseph to be presented in the Temple, was laid in the old man's arms (*Luke 2: 29-32*); now all his hopes and expectations are realised; there is nothing more for him to live for: he is ready for death. It has long been recognised that sleep is a kind of death, 'the death of each day's life', as Shakespeare called it[3], a time when we are no longer in control, when we must leave ourselves at the mercy of what the night may bring or, better, place ourselves trustfully in the hands of God. It is most appropriate that, because sleep is death-like, we are not asked to face it unless we are first armed with prayer.

Moreover, Night Prayer provides a splendid opportunity for us to express our readiness to accept bodily death whenever and however it may come. Surrender to death will be our final great act of surrender to God's will, and yet when the time arrives, we may be least able to respond as we ought: because of weariness or pain and discomfort, or confusion, or unawareness of what is impending, we may have difficulty in making a genuine act of humble submission. However, night by night we are given the opportunity to do just that: we are able to use the dying words of our Lord ('Into your hands ...') and the humble sentiments of Simeon's prayer as a way of expressing our readiness to accept the Lord's will at all times and especially in the hour of death. Now in our health and strength we prepare in advance for what is inevitably to come and what is foreshadowed by the sleep of the night ahead. After Simeon's canticle there is the concluding prayer and words of blessing: 'The Lord grant us a quiet night and a perfect end.'

The final prayer of the day is an anthem in honour of our Lady. It seems to have been in the eleventh century that Cistercian monks began the practice of processing to a statue of our Lady and singing the *Salve Regina* ('Hail, Holy Queen') at the end of Night Prayer; it was a practice which spread to the whole Church and is still followed today, though additional Anthems are also provided, especially, the *Regina Caeli* ('Queen of heaven, rejoice, Alleluia') during Eastertide. It is a moving experience to join the Cistercians, say, in their monastery at Mount St Bernard's, Leicestershire, for Night Prayer; as this final Office of the day comes to an end, the statue of Mary at the back of the nave is illuminated and everyone present, monks and visitors, turns to face it and sings the Marian anthem, with its final plea: 'After this our exile show unto us the blessed fruit of thy womb, Jesus.' Just as in the best-known prayer to Mary, we beg her to 'pray for us sinners now and (especially) at the hour of our death', so we call upon her in the same sense at the end of each day's Prayer of the Church.

Office Of Readings

Vatican II stressed the importance of the word of God, not only in preaching ('The people of God is formed .. in the first place by the living word of God' [*Decree on the Ministry & Life of Priests §4]*), but also in the liturgy ('Sacred Scripture is of the greatest importance in the celebration of the liturgy' [*CL§24*]) and for the spiritual life in general ('Christians are nourished by the word of God' [*Ministry & Life of Priests §18*]). Not surprisingly, therefore, the Prayer of the Church gives an honoured place to the reading of Scripture in each of the Hours. But the Office of Readings is so called because its distinguishing characteristic is that it consists mainly of readings from Scripture and from spiritual authors or documents of Church teaching, for it 'seeks to provide for God's people ... a wider selection of passages from sacred Scripture for meditation, together with the finest excerpts from spiritual writers' (*GI§55*). Nonetheless, it retains its character of real prayer because, as we shall see, it also includes psalms, a hymn, a prayer etc. Thus it fulfils the injunction of GI§56, which in turn quotes St Ambrose, the fourth century bishop of Milan who shepherded St Augustine into the Church: 'prayer should accompany "the reading of sacred Scripture so that there may be a conversation between God and his people" '.

This Hour, like the others, begins with the appeal: *O God, come to our aid* etc, unless it is celebrated as the first office of the day, in which case it is preceded by the Invitatory (see p.64). For contemplative monks and nuns the Office of Readings is a night office – it is comforting to know that we are being upheld by the prayers of our brothers and sisters even while we sleep – but, in accordance with the direction of CL§89, it has also been 'adapted so that it may be recited at any hour of the day'. It may even be 'anticipated', which means that tomorrow's Office of Readings can be prayed some time after Evening Prayer today, an arrangement which some people who want to follow the whole Office find particularly helpful because it fits in better with their other daily commitments. A hymn is provided for each day of the week, except on solemnities and feasts which have hymns of their own. Then come three psalms (or parts of them), with their antiphons, which are taken from the appropriate day of the current week; again, solemnities and feasts are special in that they have proper psalms and antiphons (or use one or other of the Commons of the Saints). A notable bonus of praying the Office of Readings is that it includes a number of splendid psalms, not all of which appear in other parts of the Prayer of the Church: Psalm 130 ('O Lord, my heart is not proud'), for example, which, as we have seen, is a charming song of trust in God; Psalm 135 ('O give thanks to the Lord for he is good'), the only litany in the book of psalms; Psalm 72 ('How good God is to Israel') which wrestles with the terrible problem of innocent suffering; Psalms 103 ('Bless the Lord, my soul!') and 104 ('Give thanks to the Lord, tell his name') which praise God, respectively, as Saviour and as Creator, 'twin stars of the first magnitude,' they have been called[4], in the galaxy of the psalter.

Psalms are followed by a verse and response which mark 'a transition in the prayer from psalmody to listening' (*GI§63*), for now we come to the two sets of readings which give this Hour of prayer its name. The first is always from Scripture; the original plan was to provide a two-year cycle of scriptural passages, but the idea of printing such a cycle in the breviary was abandoned, apparently because it would have made the office book too unwieldy (not to mention too expensive!). However, the one-year cycle is not as balanced as the longer course of scripture readings, and a number of important books, such as the Acts of the Apostles and Paul's letter to the Romans, do not appear at all. Care has been taken to ensure that the biblical excerpts in the Office of Readings do not duplicate those of the Mass lectionary. The latter lectionary follows a two-year cycle for weekdays and a three-year cycle for Sundays. Thus, between these readings and those which appear in the breviary, we are enabled to cover an immense tract of the bible even in the course of a single year.

The second reading might be called 'ecclesiastical' in that it is taken from 'the writings of the Fathers or Church writers, or else is a reading connected with the saints' (*GI§64*); its purpose is 'principally to provide for meditation on the word of God' (*GI§163*) and, ultimately, to lead us to 'a relish and love for (sacred Scripture)' (*GI§164*); it also offers us nourishment from a huge anthology of spiritual reflections from every age in the Church's history and from many parts of the world, east and west. Furthermore, the second readings often bring out the meaning of the seasons and feasts of the year: for example, in the weeks of Eastertide, excerpts from the writings of St Leo the Great, who was pope until 406, provide a moving commentary on the paschal mystery; or again, for the celebration of a martyr, the ecclesiastical reading may describe the spirit in which the saint went to his or her death (see, for example, in the first half of the Tenth Week in Ordinary time the excerpts from the seven moving letters which Ignatius sent to the churches in the various places he would pass on his way to Rome, where in about 110 he was put to death), or it may be taken from something that the saint of the day has written (such as a passage from the autobiography of St Thérèse of Lisieux).

Each of the readings has a heading which describes in a phrase or sentence what follows and so can be most valuable in helping us to get our bearings. Then, in order to encourage a brief prayerful reflection on the readings, each of them is followed by a response. The first of these consists of a striking phrase taken from the scripture reading, juxtaposed with another phrase taken from a biblical book which may help to bring out the full import of that reading. The second response follows a similar pattern but is not always closely linked with the text which precedes it. It is clear that the responses are meant to be sung, with one group responding to the other; but because of their potential to foster prayer, they have been retained even for individual recitation.

Finally, on solemnities and feasts, on all Sundays (except those in Lent), and on all eight days of both the Easter and Christmas octaves, the second reading is followed by the *Te Deum*, an ancient hymn – probably dating from the second century – of praise and thanksgiving; and the Hour is brought to an end with the prayer that is proper to the day and, at least in a communal celebration, with the acclamation: 'Let us praise the Lord' and the response: 'Thanks be to God.' (From earliest times it has been customary to celebrate important festivals by a vigil of prayer, the most notable of these being the Paschal Vigil. The Appendix to each volume of the full breviary makes provision for the continuation of the ancient practice on the eve of Sundays, Solemnities and Feasts: it gives three canticles and a Gospel reading which are to be added to the Office of Readings immediately before the Te Deum.)

Opening up of the Treasures[5]

Within the limits of this book it is difficult to say more about the ecclesiastical readings; apart from my own incompetence, their sheer complexity, both in terms of number as well as of style and outlook – they cover a period stretching from Pope Clement I, who died shortly before AD100, to Vatican II in the 1960s – make it impossible to do them justice. It might be said that the Scripture readings are in much the same situation, for they too were written over the course of many centuries, include many different types of writing and reflect many different outlooks. However, because they hold a unique status as the inspired word of God, they are specially deserving of our attention.

One of the criticisms that has been levelled against this Hour in the Prayer of the Church is that the inclusion of the Scripture readings in full makes the breviary extremely bulky – and unnecessarily so, for those who pray the Office of Readings will almost certainly have a bible at their disposal and will know their way around it. It would be enough, goes the argument, for the breviary to give simply a list of references to the Scripture readings (as for example some French editions of the Office do) and leave individuals to find them in their bible. It would have the additional benefit of enabling people to see the readings in their original context. Moreover, if the Jerusalem Bible were used, it would bring the added advantages of a text set out in user-friendly fashion and of invaluable footnotes.

However, whether or not the readings should appear in the breviary, I am convinced that there are few of those who pray the Office of Readings who would not be helped if a brief explanation of the readings were provided, for example, their connection with the season, their date of composition, their outstanding features, etc. It is something of that kind, though on a modest scale, that I wish to attempt in this section. (For ease of reference, you will need to keep a marker in Appendix II where the full list of scripture references is given). By way of preface, let me offer you some words which come, interestingly enough, from one of the ecclesiastical readings! St Ephrem was a fourth century monk from Syria whose hymns and voluminous writings about scripture earned him the title of Doctor of the Church. Here is his encouraging advice, in the form of a prayer, to those who persevere faithfully in scripture reading:

'Lord, who can grasp all the wealth of just one of your words? What we understand is much less than what we leave behind, like thirsty people who drink from a fountain...

The thirsty man rejoices when he drinks and he is not downcast because he cannot empty the fountain ... What, at one time, you are not able to receive because of your weakness, you will be able to receive at other times if you persevere.'

Christmas Season

In the season of Advent the scripture readings come from the prophet *Isaiah*, who lived in Jerusalem eight centuries before Jesus was born. Though what he has to say is in the first place concerned with the events and circumstances of his own day – about God's judgement on his people, about the 'remnant' who will remain faithful, about the need for penance and so on – yet he has become one of the Church's traditional Advent preachers. Nor is it difficult to understand why: after an overwhelming vision of God in the Temple, he constantly proclaims God's 'holiness' (his utter 'otherness'); at the same time, however, he speaks of God's closeness: it is Isaiah who gives us the name 'Emmanuel', God-with-us. During Advent we are preparing for the event which will bring this All Holy God among us as one of us, our Emmanuel.

During the final week of Advent, from December 17 to 24, the readings are from chapters 40 to 55 of the book of Isaiah, chapters which are often called 'Second (or Deutero-) Isaiah', because, in the view of scholars, they were written not by the prophet of that name but by another anonymous writer, imbued with his spirit, who lived a couple of centuries later, towards the end of the sixth century. In the year 586BC Jerusalem had been gutted by Nebuchadnezzar, the emperor of Babylon, and the city's population taken into exile. However, the author of Second-

Isaiah, continuing the theme of his predecessor, speaks magnificently of the glory and holiness of God, about his power to rescue his people from their Babylonian exile, about a Messiah who in a second Exodus will lead them safely home. In Advent we prepare both for Christ's coming at Christmas and for his coming at the end of time – to lead us home.

Immediately after Christmas the feasts of a number of saints occur and on the Sunday following Christmas the feast of the Holy Family, each of which has its appropriate reading. But from December 30 to January 5 the readings are taken from the letter to the *Colossians* 'which considers the incarnation of the Lord within the context of the whole history of salvation' (*GI§148*). Writing in the early 60s to the Christians at Colossae, which is situated more or less in the middle of present-day Turkey, Paul speaks inspiringly of the centrality of the 'mystery of Christ': the Child born to us at Christmastime is Someone whom we come to know ever more intimately with the passage of the years and yet will never fully understand.

The feast of the Epiphany, January 6, brings a return to Isaiah, but this time to the latter part of the book, chapters 56 to 66, known as 'Third-Isaiah' (composed, like Second-Isaiah, by an anonymous author who wrote, probably after the Babylonian exile came to an end in 538, in the spirit of the eighth-century Jerusalem prophet). It speaks of a new creation which will put an end to every ill and is obviously meant to kindle hope. There is a joyous feeling in the air, an appropriate atmosphere for the season in which we celebrate the coming of the Saviour of the World.

Easter Season

Lent sees us preparing to celebrate the paschal triduum of our Lord's death and resurrection and the readings for the first four weeks are taken from *Exodus, Leviticus* and *Numbers,* three Old Testament books which 'review the history of salvation' (*GI§150*). Exodus and Numbers in particular recall Israel's liberation from forced labour in Egypt, the first celebration of the Passover, the long exodus journey through the wilderness, when God proved himself Israel's saviour and covenant Lord, and Israel's first reconnaissance of Canaan, the promised land. Passages from the book of Leviticus – named after the tribe of Levi which played a major role in Israel's worship – have obvious links with the events the Church remembers in Holy Week, for they speak, among other things, of the consecration of the first priests and of the Day of Atonement (*Yom Kippur*), when the High Priest entered the most sacred part of the temple to offer sacrifice for the sins of the whole people. Even more striking is the connection between the Letter to the *Hebrews,* read in the final two weeks of Lent, and the events of Holy Week. This letter, written by an unknown author between AD70 and 80, was probably addressed to Jews, possibly Jewish priests, who had become Christians. It likens Christian life to another exodus – a journey to the new promised land of Heaven; but this time the leader is Jesus Christ, who in his own person replaces the priesthood of old, who through his own perfect sacrifice seals a new covenant in his blood and makes obsolete the sacrifices of former times.

The Scripture readings for the first week of Eastertide are taken from *1 Peter*, probably written towards the end of his life in the mid-sixties[6]. It seems particularly pertinent that this book should be read in the days after Easter, if, as scholars believe, it was originally a homily or liturgy for baptism, the sacrament by which we share in the dying and rising of Christ. It emphasises the dignity of the Christian vocation, as well as encouraging Christ's followers to be courageous in the face of persecution. After a further excerpt from the letter to the *Colossians* on the second Sunday of paschaltide, the readings until the end of the fifth week of Easter are taken from the *Apocalypse* (also known as Revelation), which proclaims the triumph of the risen Christ, who is King of kings and Lord of lords. It begins with a series of messages addressed to seven churches in Asia Minor (modern Turkey), assuring them of Christ's closeness to them as he offers words sometimes of comfort, sometimes of challenge and sometimes of rebuke. There follows a succession of bewildering visions – at times more like nightmares – which weave in and out of each other and make this book the most perplexing part of the New Testament. However, its first readers, persecuted Christians at the end of the first century, were familiar with this type of writing: it was used in times of crisis in order to assure God's people that all would be well, despite the apparent invincibility of their enemies and the apparent failure of God's promises. The pledge that God is in control of history, that he will utterly destroy their enemies and that their hopes of future glory are assured, that in fact the final victory has already been won – all this had to be presented in coded form for fear that it would be destroyed by the persecutors as seditious material. And so John, the author of this book, uses symbols, drawn especially from prophets such as Ezechiel, in which, for instance, 'eyes' stand for knowledge, 'horns' for power, 'white hair' for eternity, the colour 'scarlet' for majesty, and so on. Though, without a commentary, it may be difficult for us to 'crack' some of the coded visions, there should be no difficulty in finding in the book as a whole a powerful word of encouragement for ourselves who on the threshold of the third millennium face systems and values – consumerism, dependence on military might, disregard for the sanctity of life – which are no less hostile to the Christian way of life than those forces faced by our ancestors of the first century.

The final two weeks of Eastertide give us readings from the three short *Letters of John*. As might be expected, they echo many of the themes and concerns of the fourth Gospel: the relationship between the three-Personed God and the individual Christian, the need to recognise Christ as the Son of God, to walk in the light, to break with sin, to keep the commandments, especially that of love. They represent a call to live as Easter people. And the reading for Pentecost itself is the famous passage from *Romans* 8 in which Paul speaks of the transformation worked in us through the indwelling of the Spirit of God who raised Jesus from the dead, the Spirit who enables us to call upon God as Abba (Father) and urges us to live lives worthy of the glory that is to come.

'Ordinary' Time

As you will remember, Ordinary time consists of a long span of thirty-three or thirty-four weeks, running from the Monday after the feast of the Baptism of the Lord until Advent. However, the series is interrupted on Ash Wednesday, the start of Lent, and not resumed until the Monday after Pentecost Sunday, which signals the end of

Eastertide. The readings allotted to this lengthy period, unlike those of the Christmas and Easter Cycles, are not focussed on particular themes; moreover, there is such an abundant variety of passages from both the Old Testament and the New, that the best way of dealing with them may well be to take a group of readings, say, those from the historical books of the Old Testament, offer a few words of comment and then give a reference to the weeks where these works appear.

Ordinary time begins with readings from *Ecclesiasticus* (= 'church book'), also called the book of Sirach, after the name of its author ben Sirach (*Week 1*). Written about 180BC, it is one of five Old Testament books usually classified as 'wisdom literature' and deals with theoretical wisdom arising from experience, travel, listening to the wise, etc, as well as the practical wisdom passed down from parents, priests and elders concerned with right living and respect for the Law. Wisdom authors, usually building upon traditional folk-sayings, offer something approaching a philosophy of life: they speak of life's basic values, its purpose, its problems. At times the writings may seem dull, even humanistic, but they can be very striking indeed: take the book of *Job*, written some time in the sixth century BC[7], which wrestles with the intractable problem of innocent human suffering (*Weeks 8 and 9)* or the charming passage in *Ecclesiastes*, from about the third century, which proclaims that there is a time for everything – for birth and death, for planting and plucking, and so on – or the graphic description of old age in chapter 12. Job is a man of integrity who cannot be bought off with the pious clichés of his friends; he argues with God, challenges God, yet never loses hold of his belief in God: God may seem unjust but is real enough to battle and contend with. *Ecclesiastes*, also called Qoheleth (= teacher/preacher), is much bleaker than Job in its questioning (*Week 7*). It ponders on the apparent emptiness of life, lamenting in an oft-repeated refrain that 'All is vanity!' It is pessimistic, the most skeptical book in the bible, it might even be described as agnostic, and yet in asserting that there is nothing we can do (nor even anything Wisdom can offer) which will bring true and lasting happiness, is not Qoheleth at least hinting that our ultimate hope must rest in God? As its name suggests, the book of *Proverbs* (Week 6) is a collection of sayings; it was edited in its present form perhaps in the late sixth or early fifth century BC and provides instruction on how to behave in everyday life. At times it seems to rise no higher than enlightened self-interest, but a pre-Christian book cannot be expected to present gospel ideals. In fact, it does have outstanding passages which are universally appreciated, such as the fine description of the good wife, which brings the book to a close. An arresting feature of wisdom literature is that at times Wisdom speaks and is spoken of as a person: Lady Wisdom existed before anything came into being, was at God's side, a witness of his creative activity, rejoicing both in his handiwork and to be in the midst of humankind. (In speaking of Jesus in 'wisdom' terms, the earliest Christains were acknowledging that he existed with God before creation, took flesh and dwelt amongst us and continues God's saving work.) The book of *Wisdom* (*Week 30*) is the youngest of the Old Testament books, written in the century before our Lord's birth – perhaps in the last half of that century. It incorporates ideas that are familiar from earlier wisdom books, such as the praise of Lady Wisdom, but it marks a giant advance by its teaching on future life, on judgment after death and on rewards and punishments.

There is a link between wisdom literature and the book of *Deuteronomy* (*Weeks 2 and 3*). On the one hand, the purpose of the teachers of wisdom was to promote good order, based on the experiences of the past, and so they upheld the law, even identified it with wisdom; and on the other hand the purpose of Deuteronomy – its very name means 'second law' – was to bring about a return to the keeping of the law, to offer a blueprint for the moral reform which was desperately needed in Israel. In all probability it was compiled in the seventh century[8] in the form of a series of farewell discourses purportedly given by Moses before his death, but made applicable to seventh-century Israel: like their ancestors about to enter the promised land, the people must live according to the law which is itself the outcome of the covenant relationship between God and his people.

Joshua (*Week 10*) begins the history of the people of Israel after they had crossed the river Jordan and arrived in Canaan under the leadership of Moses' successor, Joshua. The conquest of Canaan is described in idealised fashion:

when the people are faithful to God they conquer, when unfaithful they are defeated. Significantly, the final chapter is devoted to a renewal of the covenant: allegiance to God is literally a matter of life and death. *Judges* (*Week 11*) serves as a reminder that the conquest was not as effortless as the previous book had suggested: it was for the most part a matter of slow infiltration with many a setback. Though concerned with the administration of justice, the 'judges' were not so much judges in our sense of the term as national heroes, raised up by God in times of crisis to deliver his people from their enemies. The Office of Readings takes up the story again in the second half of *1 Samuel* (*Weeks 12 and 13*) when young David is chosen by God to succeed Saul as king, defeats Goliath, is forced to flee the royal court because of the king's jealousy and remains an outlaw until the king's death. Then it is that David himself ascends the royal throne (*end of Week 13 and Week 14*) and we hear from *2 Samuel*, and, briefly, from *1 Chronicles*[9], the story of his reign and of his plans that his son Solomon should succeed him. His was a reign of glory but also of shame and disaster: his adultery with Bathsheba and murder of her husband Uriah, the rebellion and death of his son Absalom. A brief summary of the career of David and his successors is given (taken from *Ecclesiasticus*), and then the second half of *1 Kings* and the first chapters of *2 Kings (end of Week 14 and Week 15)* recall the powerful ministry of the ninth-century prophet Elijah, as he struggled to wean the people from the worship of the false gods (the baals) of Canaan.

It was in the next century that *Amos*, though belonging to the southern kingdom of Juda, conducted his brief ministry in the northern kingdom of Israel (*Week 18*). He is the first of the prophets whose writings have come down to us. At a time of great prosperity, he inveighed in the name of the God of justice against sleaze in high places and lack of justice for the poor. About the same time the voice of *Hosea* was also heard, once again in Israel (*Weeks 18 and beginning of 19*); drawing upon personal experience of marital breakdown, he speaks movingly of God's covenant love for his people, which is compared to that of a husband for his unfaithful wife, and pleads with the people to flee the enticing fertility cults of Canaan. Like Amos, *Micah*, a hill country farmer, roundly condemns the social injustices of his day; Israel cannot fulfil its role as hope of the world unless it is faithful to God. This is the prophet who predicted that in Bethlehem, the home town of the smallest of Israel's tribes, there would be born the saviour sent by God (*Week 19*). It was about this time – in the eighth century – that Isaiah, of whom we have already spoken, fulfilled his prophetic task in Jerusalem by reading the ominous signs of the times (*Week 20*).

By the end of the eighth century the northern kingdom had been annihilated by Assyria and in little more than a century the southern kingdom was threatened by Babylon. *Zephaniah* warns of the doom that awaits the people because of their disobedience but, like Isaiah, promises the survival of a faithful remnant (*beginning of Week 21*). About the same time, *Jeremiah,* who had been born of a priestly family a few miles north of Jerusalem, began his ministry which was to last for forty years; he threatened that despite the good times the people were enjoying, disaster would overtake them because of their unfaithfulness. He was regarded as a traitor, attempts were made on his life and the last we hear of him is when Jerusalem falls to the Babylonians and he is led off to Egypt with a group fleeing the country. Among the notable passages in Jeremiah are the account of his call and the promise of a new Covenant that God would make with his people (*Weeks 21, 22 and beginning of 23*). The author of *Lamentations* speaks of the horrors accompanying the fall of the city and the anguish of the people, though not without offering a ray of hope for the future. *Habakkuk*, another contemporary of Jeremiah, is haunted by the problem of how God can allow the ruthless Babylonians to menace his own people. The only answer he can offer is the assurance that faith will never be in vain: God is in control and can be trusted (*Week 23*).

Ezechiel, also Jeremiah's contemporary, was in the first batch of exiles to be taken to Babylon and there he remained for the rest of his life. He warned the besieged people of Jerusalem that their city would fall; but when that disaster occurred, he offered hope, especially to those in exile who felt that the Lord had deserted them. The vision of a chariot-borne God assures him that the God of Israel is a 'mobile' God, not attached to Jerusalem but able to dwell with his people in their exile. He promises they will find their hearts of stone replaced with hearts of flesh and filled with the Spirit; that they will be restored as a nation, like dry bones brought to life; that a new covenant will be struck with them and a new power to respond given them; and that the glory of God, which left Jerusalem will return and the city itself become a new Jerusalem (*Weeks 24 and 25*).

Two prophets made their appearance shortly after the return of some of the Jews from exile. *Haggai* and *Zechariah* urged them to restore Jerusalem and its ruined economy, and not to put the building of their own homes before that of the temple. Both of them, especially Zechariah, speak of a new age of blessings and messianic hope. It is a message picked up in the fifth century by *Malachi* – the name means 'my messenger' – who challenges priests and people about their religious duties and foretells the coming Day of the Lord (*Week 28*). Two fourth-century prophets also appear in the Office of Readings (*Week 33*): the first, *Joel*, brings a message of God's judgement upon all the nations but also the promise of his final victory and the pouring out of the Spirit on all his people: not surprisingly, Joel has been called the prophet of Pentecost. Finally, the latter part of *Zechariah* (in fact it seems to have been written at a later date by a disciple) speaks of the restoration of the house of David and the coming of the Messianic age, mysteriously linked with the death of an unnamed figure, 'the one whom they have pierced'.

In addition to the books of the Old Testament concerned with the Law and others with the teaching of the Prophets, there is a third miscellaneous group, usually referred to as the 'Writings'. Among them is the book of *Esther:* in guise of a short story, it tells of a plot to massacre the Jews which, thanks to the intervention of a young Jewess, backfires and leads to the destruction of the anti-semites themselves. (Among Jewish people, the triumph is celebrated to this day in the spring feast of Purim.) Another of the 'writings', dating from perhaps the same time, is attributed to a secretary of Jeremiah, *Baruch*. It treats of prayer, messianic hope, devotion to the Law, the meaning of true wisdom, the danger of idolatry (*Week 29*).

The two books of *Maccabees* recall the final Jewish struggle for freedom recorded in the Old Testament. In the late fourth century, under its charismatic leader Alexander the Great, the Greek empire had been extended as far east as India, and with it came the spread of the Greek language and civilization. Though at first Greek culture was welcomed by some Jews, by the second century it had become clear, particularly after the desecration of the temple and the beginnings of persecution, that the Jews must fight for their ancient faith. The champion of the Jewish cause was Judas Maccabeus and, after his death, his brothers (*Week 31*). As we have already seen, persecution produces its own type of literature: 'coded' messages which seem innocent enough on the surface but, for those in the know, speak of protest and defiance of the enemy. *Daniel* is one such book: though set at the time of the Babylonian exile, it in fact focusses on the situation four hundred years later, at the time of the Maccabees, when two of the great powers of the day, Greece and Egypt, fought for control of Palestine. It breathes absolute faith and trust in God, in his ability to overcome every evil empire and in the assurance that he will send One who will be king over all people and ruler of God's kingdom: it is the final expression of messianic hope to be found in the pages of the Old Testament (*Week 32*).

Of course the New Testament also features in the Office of Readings, though to a lesser degree than might have been expected: there are few passages from the letters of St Paul and none at all from the Gospels[10] . This, however, is due in large measure to the decision not to duplicate in the Office those readings already used in the Lectionary for Mass. The earliest part of the whole New Testament is *1 Thessalonians*, a letter written by Paul in about the year 50 – only twenty years after the resurrection and some twenty years before the first gospel appeared. Its four chapters offer encouragement, gratitude and exhortation to the people among whom he had lived only a few years earlier. It also deals with problems, in particular those arising from the feverish expectation that Jesus would soon return. In speaking of 'salvation through our Lord Jesus Christ who died for us', it presents the earliest New Testament statement of the redemptive nature of Christ's death. *2 Thessalonians* was probably written a few months later, clarifying and elaborating the teachings of the earlier letter (*Week 4*). *Galatians* was probably written while Paul was residing at Ephesus in about 58; to call it a 'letter' is a misnomer: it is much more a passionate defence of his position, an angry retort to those who have taught, and those who have believed, that observance of the Mosaic Law, and in particular acceptance of circumcision, is necessary for salvation. Such a view is a denial of the gospel which he had preached: salvation comes through faith in Jesus Christ, not through observance of the Law (*Week 5*).

The city of Corinth was situated on the narrow strip of land between mainland Greece and its southern peninsula; it was large, cosmopolitan and notorious. Of the letters that Paul wrote to his unruly converts there, only *2 Corinthians* is to be found in the Office of Readings – and even that may be a fusion of two or more others! (*Weeks 16 & 17*) Probably to be dated about 57, it reveals the heart of the apostle as he expresses his concern for the new Christians, strives to defend himself against 'false' apostles and recounts some of the hardships which he has endured in preaching the gospel. It was during the 50s, probably between 1 and 2 Corinthians, that Paul also wrote one of his most attractive letters, that to the *Philippians*. It is filled with a spirit of joy and affection, despite the fact that it was written from a prison cell (perhaps in Ephesus). The community he addresses are his first love in Europe, and in fact the only one from whom he was ever prepared to accept financial support. Drawing upon his own experience, he teaches his friends that Christian living is a sharing not only in the rising but also in the suffering of Christ, that their greatest glory is to 'have the mind of Christ' who humbled himself even unto death and that in all circumstances they must rejoice (*Week 26*).

Timothy was a young man when he became a disciple of Paul; later he was entrusted with charge of the church in Ephesus. He is the recipient of *1* and *2 Timothy*. Though these letters were not written by Paul himself, they do, as the Scripture scholar Raymond Brown puts it, 'preserve certain strains of genuine Pauline thought' (*Week 27*). Together with the letter to *Titus* they have been called the 'Pastoral Letters' because their main concern is with the organisation and direction of the communities for which Timothy and Titus bear responsibility.

As the Church's year draws to a close, there is a reading from the Apocalypse, in connection with the feast of Christ the King, then readings from *2 Peter* and the letter of *Jude* (*Week 34*). It is doubtful whether the first was actually written by St Peter because it seems to date from the beginning of the second century; however, by identifying himself with the prince of apostles, the author (whoever he may have been) shows that what he has to offer is apostolic teaching. He gives thanks for God's goodness, warns against errors and looks forward to the Second Coming of Christ, an event already foreshadowed in the transfiguration. The brief letter of Jude, brother of James, though originally intended, as he explains, to focus on the salvation in which he and his readers share, has had to devote itself to warning them to avoid errors and 'contend for the faith that was once for all entrusted to the saints'. And it ends with a prayer of praise:

> 'To him who is able to ... bring you faultless and joyful before his glorious presence – to the only God our Saviour, through Jesus Christ our Lord, be glory, majesty, might, and authority, from all ages past, and now, and forever and ever! Amen.'

A fitting conclusion to the Church's Year! And a splendid summary of the ultimate purpose of praying the Prayer of the Church.

'The value of the liturgy of the hours is enormous. Through it all the faithful... fulfil a role of prime importance; Christ's prayer goes on in the world. The Holy Spirit himself intercedes for God's people... In this prayer of praise we lift up our hearts to the Father ... bringing with us the anguish and hopes, the joys and sorrows of all our brothers and sisters ... Our prayer becomes a school of love – a special kind of ... love by which we love the world, but with the heart of Christ.

Through this prayer of Christ ..., our day is sanctified, our activities transformed, our actions made holy... As a community of prayer and praise, with the liturgy of the hours among the highest priorities of our day – each day – we can be sure that nothing will separate us from the love of God that is in Christ Jesus our Lord.'

(John Paul II in an address given in St Patrick's Cathedral, New York, on 3 October, 1979).

References

1. John Paul II *Tertio Millennio Adveniente* (The Coming of the Third Millennium) – the Apostolic letter in preparation for the Jubilee year 2000; Catholic Truth Society, London – §11
2. A G Martimort in *The Liturgy and Time* Liturgical Press, Collegeville, Minnesota (new ed. 1986) pp237-8
3. Macbeth II.ii
4. D Kinder *Psalms* 73-50 Inter-Varsity Press (1975) p364
5. 'The treasures of the bible are to be opened up more lavishly,' said Vatican II (*CS§51*). The reference, though specifically to the Eucharist, applies equally to the whole of the Church's liturgy.
6. Some modern scholars question the Petrine authorship of this letter, believing it to have been written towards the end of the first century AD. Even if they are right, the letter loses nothing of its significance.
7. Scholars are not agreed about its dating: most locate it in the time of the Babylonian exile, but some in the period of fear and confusion before the fall of Jerusalem in 586BC, and others in the days after the Exile when sages began to reflect on the trauma God's people had experienced.
8. However, as with the other books of the Pentateuch (the first five books of the bible), the final editing of Deuteronomy took place during the half-century of the exile, a period of intense literary activity among the Jews. The books of Joshua, Judges, Samuel and Kings, written shortly after Deuteronomy, were so influenced by its theological perspective that they are commonly referred to as 'deuteronomical history'.
9. It is generally accepted that the books of Chronicles are subsequent to the deuteronomical history (see reference 8) and represent a rewriting of history from the standpoint of Jewish priests, who wrote towards the end or more probably after the time of the exile.
10. However, in the Appendix to each volume of the three-volumed breviary, Gospel passages are allotted for the Vigils of Sundays, Solemnities and Feasts for those who wish to use them. It was customary in the early Church to preface important celebrations, such as Christmas and Pentecost, as well as Sundays, with a vigil by prolonging the Office of Readings, on analogy with the Easter Vigil. For those wishing to follow that tradition, the breviary makes provision of three canticles and a gospel reading to be added to the Office of Readings immediately before the *Te Deum*.

Glossary

Though most of these words have been explained in the text, it seemed useful to collect them together in one place for ease of reference.

Advent: The four-week season immediately before Christmas. Derived from the Latin word *adventus*, (= 'coming'), it is a time of preparation for the celebration of Christ's coming at Christmas, but also an anticipation of his Second Coming. It is a season of joy and spiritual expectation. From December 17th to 24th there are special texts each day for the eucharist and the Prayer of the Church including the 'O' Antiphons for the Magnificat.

Alleluia: A Hebrew expression which means literally 'Praise Yah(weh)', i.e. 'Praise God'. It has become a common liturgical expression of joy and so appears most frequently in Eastertide, but never during Lent.

Antiphon: A short phrase, usually from Scripture, repeated before and after a psalm or canticle, and specially chosen to highlight its key idea.

Benedictus: The first latin word of the scriptural song of Zachary, prayed in thanksgiving for the birth of his son, John the Baptist (*see Luke 1:68-79*). It is prayed at Morning Prayer after the scripture reading.

Blessing: In communal recitation, each Hour of the Prayer of the Church ends with a blessing.

Breviary: The liturgical book which contains all the texts of the Prayer of the Church.

Calendar: The General Calendar of the Church indicates the various sacred seasons which go to make up the liturgical year (see below under 'Year') and which celebrate the saving work of Christ on our behalf. It also gives the dates of the festivals of saints which are celebrated throughout the world. In addition, there are national and diocesan calendars which give the dates of festivals of more local concern, e.g. the feast of English Martyrs or the patron saint of a parish or diocese.

Canticle: From the Latin *canticulum*, which means a 'short song'. The canticles in the breviary are psalms or hymns of praise which come from Scripture but do not belong to the book of psalms. One from the Old Testament features between the two psalms at Morning Prayer, and one from the New Testament after the two psalms at Evening Prayer. While these canticles change from day to day, there are three other gospel canticles which are unchanging: the 'Benedictus' of Zachary at Morning Prayer, the 'Magnificat' of Mary at Evening Prayer and the 'Nunc Dimittis' of Simeon at Night Prayer.

Christmas, Season of: Begins on the evening of Christmas Eve and continues until the feast of the Baptism of our Lord; it is a season whose importance is second only to that of Easter.

Common: A technical term for those parts of the Liturgy of the Hours which are used for, and so are common to, a whole category of saints (e.g. martyrs, apostles) or celebrations (e.g. dedication of a church). A 'common' is opposed to a 'proper' (see below).

Divine Office: Another way of referring to the Prayer of the Church. The word 'Office' comes from the latin *officium*, which means a 'service', 'something done for another'; the 'Divine Office' is the service given to God by prayer.

Doxology: A liturgical formula of praise to God. The doxology 'Glory be to the Father...', ends each psalm.

Easter, Season of: is fifty days long, beginning on Easter Sunday and continuing until Pentecost, though it is considered one 'Great Sunday'. It has an Octave (see below).

Enumeration (of Psalms): There are slight differences in the numbering of the psalms as between the original Hebrew, which is followed by most modern Bibles, and the Greek translation, which was used by the early Church and is still in common usage in liturgical books like the breviary. In practice this means that, for the most part, the numbering of the psalms in the breviary from 10 to 145 is one behind the Hebrew numbering. That explains why the breviary regularly gives two numbers for a psalm, e.g. 130 (131), the first being its liturgical or Greek number and the second (given in brackets) its Hebrew or number.

Evening Prayer: Together with Morning Prayer, this is a pivotal Hour of the Prayer of the Church. The celebration of Sundays and Solemnities (see below) begins on the eve before, and so these days have both an Evening Prayer I and an Evening Prayer II.

Feast: A celebration next in importance to a Solemnity. There are some twenty-five feasts in the General Calendar of the Church.

Feria: A name given to an ordinary day of the week which is neither a solemnity nor a feast nor a memorial.

Hour: Refers to one of the five prayer times – formerly there were seven – that make up the Prayer of the Church, viz. Morning Prayer, Prayer(s) During the Day, Evening Prayer, Night Prayer and Office of Readings. The 'little hours' were formally known as terce, sext and none, but are now called Prayer Before Noon, Midday Prayer and Afternoon Prayer. Except in monasteries and similar religious communities, only one of these 'little hours' will usually be prayed each day.

Hymn: Hymns have featured in the Office from earliest times. Today a hymn prefaces each Hour; it is meant to set the tone and prepare the heart for the celebration about to begin. It may be omitted, e.g. if one is celebrating the Hour by oneself.

Intercessions have a place in both Morning and Evening Prayer. In the morning they take the form of praise of God and the offering to him of the new day, in the evening they are petitionary prayers for the Church and the whole human race.

Invitatory: The 'invitation' to prayer, consisting of a versicle (see below) and response, a psalm and an antiphon, with which the Divine Office begins each day.

Lauds: The former name for Morning Prayer.

Lent: This season, which lasts from Ash Wednesday to the Mass of the Lord's Supper on Holy Thursday, is a time of preparation for the celebration of Easter: catechumens are prepared for their participation in the paschal mystery through the rites of initiation, while the faithful prepare for Easter by recalling their baptism and doing penance.

Liturgy: The official public worship of the Church.

Liturgy of the Hours: Another name for the Prayer of the Church, used especially in official Church documents.

Magnificat: The first Latin word of Mary's song of praise at the Visitation (*see Luke 1:46-55*) when greeted by Elizabeth as mother of the Lord. It is prayed at Evening Prayer each day after the Scripture reading.

Mattins (also spelt 'Matins'): Though this should refer to a morning office (and it does so in the Anglican liturgy), in the Western part of the Catholic Church it is – confusingly – used of the Hour of prayer which contemplatives pray during the night hours. It is now known as the Office of Readings and can be prayed at any time of day or night.

Memorial: The lowest in the hierarchy of celebrations; it is used for most saints' days and may be obligatory or optional.

Night Prayer: The final prayer each day in the Prayer of the Church.

Nunc Dimittis: Initial words of Simeon (*see Luke 2:29-32*) as he took the child Jesus in his arms. This canticle is used daily at Night Prayer.

Octave: The period of eight days (from the Latin word *Octo* = eight) during which the celebration of a major feast is prolonged. Christmas and Easter have an Octave of celebration.

Ordinary time: In addition to the seasons of Advent, Christmas, Lent and Easter, there are thirty-three (or thirty-four) weeks in the year which do not celebrate any particular aspect of the mystery of Christ; they are referred to as the season of 'Ordinary' time.

Prayer of the Church: Another name for 'Office' or 'Liturgy of the Hours' (see above); the preferred one in this book since it emphasises that the prayer belongs to the whole Church and not exclusively to any particular group, such as the clergy, within the Church.

Proper: A technical term for those parts of the Liturgy of the Hours which belong to a particular season of the Church's Year, e.g. Christmastide, or a particular saint's day.

Readings (office of): An Hour of the Prayer of the Church which may be celebrated at any time, night or day. Its outstanding feature are the two readings – the first from Scripture, the second from an ecclesiastical source, such as the writings of one of the saints or an official church document – which follow the psalms.

Psalm: The word, originally Greek, means a song sung to a musical instrument. It is used of the one hundred and fifty songs that make up the book of Psalms and play a central role in the Prayer of the Church. Songs that do not fall within the Psalter (the collection of 150) are usually called canticles.

Psalter: The collection of psalms (see above). In the Prayer of the Church three of the collection (psalms 57, 82 and 108) are omitted entirely because of their curses (and some verses of certain psalms have been omitted for a similar reason); three others (77, 104 and 105) are reserved for the seasons of Advent, Christmas, Lent and Easter; all the rest are distributed over a four-week cycle; however, on the first Sundays of Advent, Lent, Easter and Ordinary time the cycle begins again with the psalms of Week One.

Responsory: From the Latin *respondere,* which means 'to answer'. It is a series of versicles (see below) and responses (see below under versicles) which answer each other. A good example is to be found in the Short Responsory which follows the Scripture Reading at Morning and Evening Prayer.

Solemnity: The most important type of celebration; it has its own proper office and begins at Evening Prayer of the previous day with a Vespers I. There are only fifteen solemnities in the General Calendar of the Church.

Sunday: The day of the Lord, beginning with Evening Prayer I, is the Church's weekly celebration of the Resurrection; it takes precedence over all other celebrations except those which rank as Solemnities or Feasts of the Lord. However, the Sundays of Advent, Lent and the Easter season have an absolute priority.

Te Deum: From the latin *Te Deum laudamus* = we praise you, O Lord. An ancient hymn of thanksgiving recited at the end of the Office of Readings on Sundays (except in Lent), solemnities and feasts.

Terce, Sext and None: traditional names for parts of the office, in accordance with the time of day at which they are celebrated, i.e. the third hour (in the course of the morning), the sixth hour (at midday) and the ninth hour (in the afternoon). They are now known as 'Prayer before Noon', 'Midday Prayer' and 'Afternoon Prayer'. If only one of these offices is celebrated, the psalm is that given for the particular day of the week; if all three are celebrated, the other psalms should be taken from the complementary psalmody.

Triduum: The name given to a celebration which lasts for three days, in particular to the Easter, or Paschal, Triduum, which begins with the Evening Mass of Holy Thursday night, reaches its high point in the Easter Vigil and closes with Evening Prayer on Easter Sunday. This triduum constitutes the culmination of all the Church's liturgical celebrations.

Versicle: From the latin word *versiculus*, meaning 'little verse'; it is used for the brief phrase or sentence which forms the first part of a Responsory (see above), and is 'answered' by the response. Thus: 'Lord, open my lips' is a versicle, while 'And my lips will declare your praise' is the response.

Vespers: The former name for Evening Prayer.

Vigil: It was customary in the early Church to preface important celebrations, such as Christmas and Pentecost, with a vigil by prolonging the Office of Readings, on analogy with the Easter Vigil. Provision is made in the Appendix to the three-volumed breviary to extend this ancient custom on the eves of Sundays, Solemnities and feasts by the addition of three canticles and a Gospel reading immediately before the *Te Deum* in the Office of Readings.

Year, Liturgical (also Church's Year): The celebration throughout the course of the year, of the entire saving work of Christ, and also of the feasts of Mary and the Saints whose lives proclaim the wonderful works of God, above all of his paschal triumph.

Appendix I

The following diagrams show at a glance the psalms which are prayed each day throughout the four-week cycle. Normally three psalms are allotted to each Hour, though at Morning and Evening Prayer one of them is a canticle, i.e. a psalm which comes not from the psalter but from some other part of the Bible. Sometimes a long psalm is divided into two or three parts, indicated here by the numerals I, II and III. However, where such a psalm is divided not simply within one Hour but over one or more Hours (see especially Psalm 118), this is indicated by superscripts a, b, c etc.

The three 'historical' psalms 77, 104 and 105, which unfold the way in which the history of salvation in the Old Testament is fulfilled in the New, are reserved for the Hour of Readings on the Saturdays of Advent, Christmastide, Lent and Easter.

WEEK ONE

	Morning Prayer			Prayer during day			Evening Prayer			Readings		
		CANTICLE							CANTICLE			
Sun	62		149	117I	117II	117III	109	113^a		1	2	3
Mon	5		28	18^b	7I	7II	10	14		6	9^aI	9^aII
Tue	23		32	118^a	12	13	19	20		9^bI	9^bII	11
Wed	35		46	118^b	16I	16II	26I	26II		17^aI	17^aII	17^aIII
Thur	56		47	118^c	24I	24II	29	31		17^bI	17^bII	17^bIII
Fri	50		99	118^d	25	27	40	45		34I	34II	34III
Sat	118^o		116	118^e	33I	33II	118	15		130	131I	131II

WEEK TWO

	Morning Prayer			Prayer during day			Evening Prayer			Readings		
Sun	117	CANTICLE	150	22	75I	75II	109	113^{b}	CANTICLE	103I	103II	103III
Mon	41		18a	118^{f}	39I	39II	44I	44II		30I	30II	30III
Tue	42		64	118^{g}	52	53	48I	48II		36I	36II	36III
Wed	76		96	118^{h}	54I	54II	61	66		38I	38II	51
Thur	79		80	118^{i}	55	56	71I	71II		43I	43II	43III
Fri	50		147	118^{j}	58	59	114	120		37I	37II	37III
Sat	91		8	118^{k}	60	63	112	115		135I	135II	135III

WEEK THREE

	Morning Prayer			Prayer during day			Evening Prayer			Readings		
Sun	92	CANTICLE	148	117I	117II	117III	109	110	CANTICLE	144I	144II	144III
Mon	83		95	118^{l}	70I	70II	122	123		49I	49II	49III
Tue	84		66	118^{m}	73I	73II	124	130		67I	67II	67III
Wed	85		97	118^{n}	69	74	126	126		88^{a}I	88^{a}II	88^{a}III
Thur	86		98	118°	78	79	131I	131II		88^{b}I	88^{b}II	89
Fri	50		99	21I	21II	21III	134I	134II		68I	68II	68III
Sat	118		116	118^{p}	33I	33II	121	129		106I	106II	106III

WEEK FOUR

	Morning Prayer			Prayer during day			Evening Prayer			Readings		
Sun	117	CANTICLE	150	22	75I	75II	109	111	CANTICLE	23	65I	65II
Mon	89		134	118^{q}	81	119	135I	135II		72I	72II	72III
Tue	100		143a	118^{r}	87I	87II	136	137		101I	101II	101III
Wed	107		145	118^{s}	93I	93II	138I	138II		102I	102II	102III
Thur	142		146	118^{t}	127	128	143I	143II		43I	43II	43III
Fri	50		147	118^{u}	132	139	144I	144II		54I	54II	54III
Sat	91		8	118^{v}	44I	44II	140	141		49I	49II	49III

Night Prayer normally has one psalm, though occasionally two. Moreover, the Night Prayer psalms are the same each week throughout the four-week cycle.

	Night Prayer	
Sun	90	→
Mon	85	→
Tue	142	→
Wed	30	129
Thur	15	→
Fri	87	→
Sat	4	133

Appendix II

Advent

Week I

Sunday	Isaiah 1:1-18
Monday	Isaiah 1:21-27; 2:1-5
Tuesday	Isaiah 2:6-22; 4:2-6
Wednesday	Isaiah 5:1-7
Thursday	Isaiah 16:1-5; 17:4-8
Friday	Isaiah 19:16-25
Saturday	Isaiah 21:6-12

Week II

Sunday	Isaiah 22:8b-23
Monday	Isaiah 24:1-18a
Tuesday	Isaiah 24:19-25:5
Wednesday	Isaiah 25:6-26:6
Thursday	Isaiah 26:7-21
Friday	Isaiah 27:1-13
Saturday	Isaiah 29:1-8

Week III

Sunday	Isaiah 29:13-24
Monday	Isaiah 30:18-26
Tuesday	Isaiah 30:27-33; 31:4-9
Wednesday	Isaiah 31:1-3; 32:1-8
Thursday	Isaiah 32:15-33:6
Friday	Isaiah 33:7-24

December 17th-24th

17th	Isaiah 45:1-13
18th	Isaiah 46:1-13
19th	Isaiah 47:3b-15
20th	Isaiah 48:1-11
21st	Isaiah 48:12-21;49:9b-13
22nd	Isaiah 49:14-50:1
23rd	Isaiah 51:1-11
24th	Isaiah 51:17-52:2, 7-10

Christmas

25th	Isaiah 11:1-10
H. Family*	Ephesians 5:21-6,4
26th Stephen	Acts 6:8-7:2a,44-59
27th John	1 John:1-2:3
28th	
H Innocents	Exodus 1:8- 16,22
29th	Colossians 1:1-14
30th	Colossians 1:15-2:3
31st	Colossians 2:4-15
1st Jan:	Hebrews 2:9-17
2nd Jan:	Colossians 2:16-3:4
3rd Jan:	Colossians 3:5-16
4th Jan:	Colossians 3:17-4:1
5th Jan:	Colossians 4:2-18
6th Jan:	Isaiah 42:1-8
7th Jan:	Isaiah 61:1-11

Week after January 1st

Sunday	Isaiah 60:1-22
Monday	Isaiah 61:1-11
Tuesday	Isaiah 62:1-12
Wednesday	Isaiah 63:7-19
Thursday	Isaiah 63:19-64:11
Friday	Isaiah 65:13-25
Saturday	Isaiah 66:10-14, 18-23

Baptism of the Lord

Isaiah 42:1-9; 49:1-9

Lent

Ash W	Isaiah 58:1-12
Thursday	Exodus 1:1-22
Friday	Exodus 2:1-22
Saturday	Exodus 3:1-20

Sunday I

Sunday	Exodus 5:1-6:1
Monday	Exodus 6:2-13
Tuesday	Exodus 6:29-7:25
Wednesday	Exodus 10:21-11:10
Thursday	Exodus 12:1-20
Friday	Exodus 12:21-36
Saturday	Exodus 12:37-49;13:11-16

Sunday II

Sunday	Exodus 13:17-14:9
Monday	Exodus 14:10-31
Tuesday	Exodus 16:1-18; 35
Wednesday	Exodus 17:1-16
Thursday	Exodus 18:13-27
Friday	Exodus19:1-19; 20:18-21
Saturday	Exodus 20:1-17

Sunday III

Sunday	Exodus 22:20-23:9
Monday	Exodus 24:1-18
Tuesday	Exodus 32:1-20
Wednesday	Exodus 33:7-11, 18-23; 34:5-9; 29-35
Thursday	Exodus 34:10-28
Friday	Exodus 35:30-36:1; 37:1-9
Saturday	Exodus 40:16-38

Sunday IV

Sunday	Leviticus 8:1-17;9:22-24
Monday	Leviticus 16:2-28
Tuesday	Leviticus 19:1-18;31-37
Wednesday	Numbers 11:4-6, 10-30
Thursday	Numbers 13:1-3,17-33
Friday	Numbers 14:1-25
Saturday	Numbers 20:1-13; 21:4-9

Sunday V

Sunday	Hebrews 1:1-2:4
Monday	Hebrews 2:5-18
Tuesday	Hebrews 3:1-19
Wednesday	Hebrews 6:9-20
Thursday	Hebrews 7:1-11
Friday	Hebrews 7:11-28
Saturday	Hebrews 8:1-13

Holy Week

Sunday	Hebrews 10:1-18
Monday	Hebrews 10:19-39
Tuesday	Hebrews 12:1-13
Wednesday	Hebrews 12:14-29
Thursday	Hebrews 4:14-5:10
Friday	Hebrews 9:11-28
Saturday	Hebrews 4:1-16

Eastertide

Monday	1 Peter 1:1-21
Tuesday	1 Peter 1:22-2:10
Wednesday	1 Peter 2:11-25
Thursday	1 Peter 3:1-17
Friday	1 Peter 3:18-4:11
Saturday	1 Peter 4:12-5:14

Easter II

Sunday	Colossians 3:1-17
Monday	Revelation 1:1-20
Tuesday	Revelation 2:1-11
Wednesday	Revelation 2:12-29
Thursday	Revelation 3:1-22
Friday	Revelation 4:1-11
Saturday	Revelation 5:1-14

Easter III

Sunday	Revelation 6:1-17
Monday	Revelation 7:1-17
Tuesday	Revelation 8:1-13
Wednesday	Revelation 9:1-12
Thursday	Revelation 9:13-21
Friday	Revelation 10:1-11
Saturday	Revelation 11:1-19

Easter IV

Sunday	Revelation 12:1-18
Monday	Revelation 13:1-18
Tuesday	Revelation 14:1-13
Wednesday	Revelation 14:14-15:4
Thursday	Revelation 15:5-16:21
Friday	Revelation 17:1-18
Saturday	Revelation 18:1-20

Easter V

Sunday	Revelation 18:21-19:10
Monday	Revelation 19:11-21
Tuesday	Revelation 20:1-15
Wednesday	Revelation 21:1-8
Thursday	Revelation 21:9-27
Friday	Revelation 22:1-9
Saturday	Revelation 22:10-21

Easter VI

Sunday	1 John 1:1-10
Monday	1 John 2:1-11
Tuesday	1 John 2:12-17
Wednesday	1 John 2:18-29
Ascension	Ephesians 4:1-24
Friday	1 John 3:1-10
Saturday	1 John 3:11-17

Easter VII

Sunday	1 John 3:18-24
Monday	1 John 4:1-10
Tuesday	1 John 4:11-21
Wednesday	1 John 5:1-12
Thursday	1 John 5:13-21
Friday	2 John
Saturday	3 John

Pentecost

Sunday	Romans 8:5-27

Ordinary Time

Week I

Monday	Ecclesiasticus 1:1-20
Tuesday	Ecclesiasticus 11:12-28
Wednesday	Ecclesiasticus 24:1-22
Thursday	Ecclesiasticus 42:15-43:12
Friday	Ecclesiasticus 43:13-32
Saturday	Ecclesiasticus 44:1-2,16-45:5

Week II

Sunday Deuteronomy 1:1,6-18
Monday Deuteronomy 4:1-8,32-40
Tuesday Deuteronomy 6:4-25
Wednesday Deuteronomy 7:6-14;8:1-6
Thursday Deuteronomy 9:7-21, 25-29
Friday Deuteronomy 10:12-11:9, 26-28
Saturday Deuteronomy 16:1-17

Week III

Sunday Deuteronomy 18:1-22
Monday Deuteronomy 24:1-25:4
Tuesday Deuteronomy 26:1-19
Wednesday Deuteronomy 29:1-5,9-28
Thursday Deuteronomy 30:1-20
Friday Deuteronomy 31:1-15,23
Saturday Deuteronomy 32:48-52; 34:1-12

Week IV

Sunday 1 Thessalonians 1:1-2:12
Monday 1 Thessalonians 2:13-3:13
Tuesday 1 Thessalonians 4:1-18
Wednesday 1 Thessalonians 5:1-28
Thursday 2 Thessalonians 1:1-12
Friday 2 Thessalonians 2:1-17
Saturday 2 Thessalonians 3:1-18

Week V

Sunday Galatians 1:1-12
Monday Galatians 1:13-2:10
Tuesday Galatians 2:11-3:14
Wednesday Galatians 3:15-4:7
Thursday Galatians 4;8-5:1
Friday Galatians 5:1b-25
Saturday Galatians 5:25-6:18

Week VI

Sunday Proverbs 1:1-7,20-33
Monday Proverbs 3:1-20
Tuesday Proverbs 8:1-5,12-36
Wednesday Proverbs 9:1-18
Thursday Proverbs 10:6-32
Friday Proverbs 25:1-28
Saturday Proverbs 31:10-31

Week VII

Sunday Ecclesiastes 1:1-18
Monday Ecclesiastes 2:1-26
Tuesday Ecclesiastes 3:1-23
Wednesday Ecclesiastes 5:9-6:8
Thursday Ecclesiastes 7:1-8:1
Friday Ecclesiastes 8:5-9:10
Saturday Ecclesiastes 11:7-12:14

Week VIII

Sunday Job 1:1-22
Monday Job 2:1-13
Tuesday Job 3:1-26
Wednesday Job 7:1-21
Thursday Job 11:1-20
Friday Job 12:1-25
Saturday Job 13:13-14:6

Week IX

Sunday Job 28:1-28
Monday Job 29:1-10; 30:1,9-23
Tuesday Job 31:1-23,35-37
Wednesday Job 32:1-6; 33:1-22
Thursday Job 38:1-30
Friday Job 40:6-24
Saturday Job 42:7-17

Week X

Sunday Ecclesiasticus 46:1-10
Monday Joshua 1:1-18
Tuesday Joshua 2:1-24
Wednesday Joshua 3:1-17; 4:14-19; 5:10-12
Thursday Joshua 5:13-6:21
Friday Joshua 10:1-14,11:15-17
Saturday Joshua 24:1-7,13-28

Week XI

Sunday Judges 2:6-3:4
Monday Judges 4:1-24
Tuesday Judges 6:1-6,11-24
Wednesday Judges 6:33-40; 7:1-8, 16-22a
Thursday Judges 8:22-23,30-32; 9:1-15,19-20
Friday Judges 13:1-25
Saturday Judges 16:4-6,16-31

Week XII

Sunday 1 Samuel 16:1-13
Monday 1 Samuel 17:1-10,32, 38-51a
Tuesday 1 Samuel 17:57-18:9, 20-30
Wednesday 1 Samuel 19:8-10; 20:1-17
Thursday 1 Samuel 21:1-9; 22:1-5
Friday 1 Samuel 25:14-24a, 28-39a
Saturday 1 Samuel 26:5-25

Week XIII

Sunday	1 Samuel 28:3-25
Monday	1 Samuel 31:1-4; 2 Samuel 1:1-16
Tuesday	2 Samuel 2:1-11; 3:1-5
Wednesday	2 Samuel 4:2-5:7
Thursday	2 Samuel 6:1-23
Friday	2 Samuel 7:1-25
Saturday	2 Samuel 11:1-17,26-27

Week XIV

Sunday	2 Samuel 12:1-25
Monday	2 Samuel 15:7-14,24-30; 16:5-13
Tuesday	2 Samuel 18:6-17,24- 19:4
Wednesday	2 Samuel 24:1-4,10-18, 24b-25
Thursday	1 Chronicles 22:5-19
Friday	1 Kings 1:11-35; 2:10-12
Saturday	Ecclesiasticus 47:12-25

Week XV

Sunday	1 Kings 16:29-17:16
Monday	1 Kings 18:16b-40
Tuesday	1 Kings 19:1-9a,11-21
Wednesday	1 Kings 21:1-21,27-29
Thursday	1 Kings 22:1-9, 15-23,29, 34-38
Friday	2 Chronicles 20:1-9, 13-24
Saturday	2 Kings 2:1-15

Week XVI

Sunday	2 Corinthians 1:1-14
Monday	2 Corinthians 1:15-2:11
Tuesday	2 Corinthians 2:12-3:6
Wednesday	2 Corinthians 3:7-4:4
Thursday	2 Corinthians 4:5-18
Friday	2 Corinthians 5:1-21
Saturday	2 Corinthians 6:1-7:1

Week XVII

Sunday	2 Corinthians 7:2-16
Monday	2 Corinthians 8:1-24
Tuesday	2 Corinthians 9:1-15
Wednesday	2 Corinthians 10:1-11:6
Thursday	2 Corinthians 11:7-29
Friday	2 Corinthians 11:30-12:13
Saturday	2 Corinthians 12:14-13:13

Week XVIII

Sunday	Amos 1:1-2:3
Monday	Amos 2:4-16
Tuesday	Amos 7:1-17
Wednesday	Amos 9:1-15
Thursday	Hosea 1:1-9; 3:1-5
Friday	Hosea 2:4a,10-25
Saturday	Hosea 5:15b-7:2

Week XIX

Sunday	Hosea 11:1-11
Monday	Hosea 14:2-10
Tuesday	Micah 3:1-12
Wednesday	Micah 4:1-7
Thursday	Micah 4:14-5:7
Friday	Micah 6:1-15
Saturday	Micah 7:7-20

Week XX

Sunday	Isaiah 6:1-13
Monday	Isaiah 3:1-15
Tuesday	Isaiah 7:1-17
Wednesday	Isaiah 9:7-10:4
Thursday	Isaiah 11:1-16
Friday	Isaiah 30:1-18
Saturday	Isaiah 37:21-35

Week XXI

Sunday	Zephaniah 1:1-7,14-2:3
Monday	Zephaniah 3:8-20
Tuesday	Jeremiah 1:1-19
Wednesday	Jeremiah 2:1-13,20-25
Thursday	Jeremiah 3:1-5,19-4:4
Friday	Jeremiah 4:5-8,13-28
Saturday	Jeremiah 7:1-20

Week XXII

Sunday	Jeremiah 11:18-20; 12:1-13
Monday	Jeremiah 19:1-5,10-20:6
Tuesday	Jeremiah 20:7-18
Wednesday	Jeremiah 26:1-15
Thursday	Jeremiah 29:1-14
Friday	Jeremiah 30:18-31:9
Saturday	Jeremiah 31:15-22,27-34

Week XXIII

Sunday	Jeremiah 37:21; 38:14-28
Monday	Jeremiah 42:1-16; 43:4-7
Tuesday	Habakkuk 1:1-2:4
Wednesday	Habakkuk 2:5-20
Thursday	Lamentations 1:1-12,18-20
Friday	Lamentations 3:1-33
Saturday	Lamentations 5:1-22

Week XXIV

Sunday	Ezekiel 1:3-14, 22-28
Monday	Ezekiel 2:8-3:11,16-21
Tuesday	Ezekiel 8:1-6,16-9:11
Wednesday	Ezekiel 10:18-22; 11:14-25
Thursday	Ezekiel 12:1-16
Friday	Ezekiel 16:3,5b,6-7a, 8-15,35,37a,40-43, 59-63
Saturday	Ezekiel 18:1-13,20-32

Week XXV

Sunday	Ezekiel 24:15-27
Monday	Ezekiel 34:1-6,11-16, 23-31
Tuesday	Ezekiel 36:16-36
Wednesday	Ezekiel 37:1-14
Thursday	Ezekiel 37:15-28
Friday	Ezekiel 40:1-4; 43:1-12; 44:6-9
Saturday	Ezekiel 47:1-12

Week XXVI

Sunday	Philippians 1:1-11
Monday	Philippians 1:12-26
Tuesday	Philippians 1:27-2:11
Wednesday	Philippians 2:12-30
Thursday	Philippians 3;1-16
Friday	Philippians 3:17-4:9
Saturday	Philippians 4:10-23

Week XXVII

Sunday	1 Timothy 1:1-20
Monday	1 Timothy 2:1-15
Tuesday	1 Timothy 3:1-16
Wednesday	1 Timothy 4:1-5:2
Thursday	1 Timothy 5:3-25
Friday	1 Timothy 6:1-10
Saturday	1 Timothy 6:11-21

Week XXVIII

Sunday	Haggai 1:1-2:10
Monday	Haggai 2:11-23
Tuesday	Zechariah 1:1-2:4
Wednesday	Zechariah 3:1-4:14
Thursday	Zechariah 8:1-17,20-23
Friday	Malachi 1:1-14; 2:13-16
Saturday	Malachi 3:1-24

Week XXIX

Sunday	Esther 1:1-3,9-14,16,19; 2:5-10,16-17
Monday	Esther 3:1-15
Tuesday	Esther 4:1-17
Wednesday	Esther 4:17k-14z
Thursday	Esther 5:1-8; 7-1-10
Friday	Baruch 1:14-2:5; 3:1-8
Saturday	Baruch 3:9-15,24-4:4

Week XXX

Sunday	Wisdom 1:15
Monday	Wisdom 1:16-2:1a,10-25
Tuesday	Wisdom 3:1-19
Wednesday	Wisdom 6:1-27
Thursday	Wisdom 7:15-30
Friday	Wisdom 8:1-21b
Saturday	Wisdom 11:21b-12:2, llb-19

Week XXXI

Sunday	1 Maccabees 1:1-25
Monday	1 Maccabees 1:41-64
Tuesday	1 Maccabees2:1,15-28, 42-50, 65-70
Wednesday	1 Maccabees 3:1-26
Thursday	1 Maccabees 4:36-59
Friday	2 Maccabees 12:32-45
Saturday	1 Maccabees 9:1-22

Week XXXII

Sunday	Daniel 1:-1-21
Monday	Daniel 2:26-47
Tuesday	Daniel 3:8-13,19b-24, 91-97
Wednesday	Daniel 5:1-2,5-9, 13-17, 25-31
Thursday	Daniel 9:1-4a,18-27
Friday	Daniel 10:1-21
Saturday	Daniel 12:1-13

Week XXXIII

Sunday	Joel 2:21-32
Monday	Joel 3:1-3.9-21
Tuesday	Zechariah 9:1,10:2
Wednesday	Zechariah 10:3-11:3
Thursday	Zechariah 11:4-12:8
Friday	Zechariah12:9-12a; 13:1-9
Saturday	Zechariah 14:1-21

Week XXXIV

Christ the King	
	Revelation1:4-6,10, 12-18; 2:26,28; 3:5 12,20-21
Monday	2 Peter 1:1-11
Tuesday	2 Peter 1:12-21
Wednesday	2 Peter 2:1-9
Thursday	2 Peter 2:9-22
Friday	2 Peter 3:1-18
Saturday	Jude 1-8,12-13,17-25

* This feast is celebrated on the Sunday within the Octave of Christmas, except when Christmas day falls on Sunday in which case the Holy Family is celebrated on 30 December.

By the same author

NEW LIGHT

Discovering the Psalms in the Prayer of the Church

by Richard Atherton

£7.95

This book combines scholarship and a friendly comfortable style. The first part takes the reader through the history of the psalms, showing how to spot the different types of psalms and how to use and understand the more "difficult" ones.

The second half of the book follows the Psalter day by day. An explanation of the significance and the relevance of each psalm is given as and when it occurs in the Psalter.

This is a book which is a valuable resource for all who pray the Prayer of the Church and for anyone who is interested in the tradition of prayer and the psalms we encounter in Scripture.

PRAYER OF THE CHURCH

Divine Office I
Advent, Christmastide, Weeks 1-9 **£45**

Divine Office II
Lent and Eastertide, **£45**

Divine Office III
Weeks of the Year 6-34 **£45**

Morning and Evening Prayer **£25**

Shorter Morning and Evening Prayer **£8.99**

Documents of Vatican II
Austin Flannery, O.P.
Vol. I **£17.99**
Vol. II **£11.99**